PRINT AND PRODUCTION
FINISHES FOR PACKAGING

A RotoVision Book

Published and distributed by RotoVision SA
Route Suisse 9
CH-1295 Mies
Switzerland

RotoVision SA
Sales and Editorial Office
Sheridan House, 114 Western Road
Hove BN3 1DD, UK

Tel: +44 (0)1273 72 72 68
Fax: +44 (0)1273 72 72 69
www.rotovision.com

10 9 8 7 6 5 4 3 2 1

ISBN: 978-2-940361-97-7

Art Director: Tony Seddon
Design: Morris and Winrow
Photography: Simon Punter

Reprographics in Singapore by ProVision Pte.
Tel: +65 6334 7720
Fax: +65 6334 7721

Printed in Singapore by Star Standard Industries (Pte.) Ltd.

PRINT AND PRODUCTION FINISHES FOR PACKAGING

EDWARD DENISON

RotoVision

CONTENTS

INTRODUCTION

Often banal, sometimes brilliant, and occasionally groundbreaking, packaging—as nearly everything we buy is packaged—is an aspect of design that we encounter more than almost any other. Influencing heavily the content of this endless stream of items is the form, appearance, and style of the packaging. Design lies at the heart of this process, and its successful outcome depends on the expertise of both the structural designer and the graphic designer and the effectiveness of their vital interrelationship. For both of these specialisms to accomplish their objectives they depend on two distinct processes—the structural designer on manufacturing and the graphic designer on printing. While the physical and visual characteristics of the package perform necessary practical roles, the chosen finish that each can provide imparts visual, tactile, and sensuous qualities that can excite, intrigue, and assist the user. Commercially, the effective combination of these processes can even mean the difference between spectacular success and failure.

Printing finishes deliver important visual messages by representing the product textually, graphically, or photographically, but they can also enliven the appearance of the presentation and enhance the way in which the visual elements integrate with one another, and they are critical to the way in which the product is perceived by the user. As printing technologies are constantly improved and new innovations perfected, the graphic designer can choose from an ever expanding range of printing finishes to achieve the desired appearance and performance of the package—from the standard four-color processes to special finishes such as metallic inks, holographic printing, lamination, foil blocking, varnishing, and overprinting. Foremost in influencing the choice of printing finish is the material itself. The range of paper stock available to designers working with fiberboard is bewildering, and the different coatings, lamination, board types and weights will impact significantly on the final appearance of the job. Equally, using metal, plastic, glass, or other less common packaging materials requires special attention when considering printing options. In these cases, printing is often applied either directly to the material or to a secondary material that is affixed to the package through an adhesive label, heat-shrunk sleeve, or tag.

While different effects can be achieved on different packaging materials through printing, the type of manufacturing process presents even more choice for the packaging designer. Depending on the type of material, all manner of different finishes can be achieved by processes such as embossing, debossing, die-cutting, stamping, molding, and etching. These production processes can be applied to the packaging material in a way that alters the entire surface texture or enhances specific details, but it is when they are used together with printing that the full extent of finishing opportunities available to the packaging designer is truly realized. For example, spot varnishing and embossing are often used concurrently to visually and physically lift a detail from the surface of the package, just as the shape and position of a die-cut window in a carton is often influenced by the printed design framing it.

The combination of printing and production finishes offers virtually no limit to the range and extent of finishes that can be achieved, but the designer should remain vigilant to the environmental cost of this choice. Printing and production finishes are at times misconstrued as being superfluous, since their role is often directed at adding value rather than meaning to a package. In an age where environmentally conscious design is not simply experiencing a resurgence but its future role is imperative, the packaging designer's choice of printing and production techniques should always consider the environmental impact of a design. For example, the excessive use of materials and inks leads to unnecessary wastage, both in the packaging itself and in the manufacturing and transportation of the materials and inks. Equally, the types of materials and printing finishes should, where possible, impact as little as possible on the environment while achieving their desired finish. Nearly all packaging materials are recyclable, and many are made from recycled material, just as many modern inks and other printing finishes are manufactured from nontoxic ingredients, which was not the case in the past. These improvements and innovations will continue to deliver lasting benefits to the packaging industry and to the environment if designers continue to use them. Where possible, attention has been drawn to the environmental benefits of the printing and production processes in the case studies discussed in this book.

The selection of case studies aims to present a wide range of packaging finishes used in different scenarios from across the industry and throughout the world that either employ printing finishes, production finishes, or both— from the common to the unique, from the simple to the complex, and from the cost effective to the lavish. The choice of samples is not intended to be exhaustive, nor can it be. Rather, the aim is to offer a broad collection of case studies that inspire, inform, and motivate designers engaged in packaging and thereby help stimulate future design projects.

Finally, it is worth mentioning that packaging, unlike other fields of design that draw on the combined skills of the graphic and industrial designer, presents a unique challenge since it encompasses such a diversity of materials and production processes. The range of finishes that can be achieved through the choice of printing or production techniques present extensive creative opportunities, but they are invariably constrained by the packaging material. This is often, but not always, predetermined before the design brief has been set—a detergent manufacturer is as unlikely to invest time and effort in designing fancy glass packaging as a tissue-paper producer is to indulge in packaging its product in steel boxes. This book has acknowledged this constraint in the way it has been structured by representing case studies according to material rather than print or production technique.

GLORIOUS GLASS

Glass is one of the oldest packaging materials known, and to this day remains one of the most alluring as its unique characteristics give it an eminent quality that is glorious and surprisingly versatile. It has been used in packaging for over three millennia, and humans have been blowing glass to make containers for 2,000 years, but today glass can be formed into almost any shape, colored in an infinite range of hues, and mass produced in processes that manufacture millions of containers every day. The versatility of glass as a packaging material can be seen in the extraordinary range of applications for which it is used—from a bottle of beer to an exquisitely cut crystal decanter, or from table wine to luxury perfume, glass can perform the most basic packaging function or deliver unrivaled excellence. Environmentally, glass also boasts excellent characteristics. Since its base material is sand it is nontoxic if disposed of, but, far better still, it is extremely easy to reuse and recycle.

DRAGON

Project
Ballantine's bottle and carton

Design
Creative Partner **Samantha Dumont**
Design Director **Chris Barber**
Designer **Oliver Bedwell**
Production Manager **John Cox**

Client
Pernod Ricard

Specification
Cartonboard, pressure-sensitive label, foil blocking, satin silver ink, halftone overprinting, embossing, offset lithography, lacquer varnish

Maintaining the strong brand presence of a distinguished product in a global marketplace is a major challenge for structural and graphic designers. The subtle redesign of this glass bottle and labeling utilized a range of finishes to successfully develop the brand's customer appeal and premium values in an international context. The glass bottle, with its broad facade, wide shoulders, and pronounced neck, projects a confident and sincere appearance that is augmented by the linear arrangement of printed labels and the distinctive pewter coin. The labels display the product logo and title clearly, using foil and satin silver printing to lift certain details from the various motifs, such as the elaborate crest and the labels' edging. Consideration for a broad range of different user environments has resulted in careful attention to detail in the labels' overall finish: a lacquer coating applied to the label not only enhances its appearance, but also makes it particularly conspicuous when lit with ultraviolet light such as that frequently used in bars or nightclubs. Printing finishes are vital in providing a premium feel to the secondary packaging, which comprises a litho-printed carton-board container. The product logo has been blind embossed on the side of the carton, while satin silver inks and halftone overprinting significantly improve the appearance of subtle elements such as the embossed coin.

The overall distinction of both the bottle and the carton is amplified by the coin device, which was achieved comparatively simply on the carton through printing and embossing, but which required rigorous testing before a suitable design solution for the bottle was found. The resulting pressure-sensitive label has been printed with subtle halftones to give the coin its graphic detailing, while a tactile varnish provides a subtly embossed feel to match the physical and visual elegance of the corresponding device on the carton.

PAUL CARTWRIGHT BRANDING

Project
Kirsty McLeod Skincare bottles and boxes

Design
Designer **Paul Cartwright**
Project Manager **Belinda Roberts at Snowbell**
Printing **Lumson, Italy (bottles and jars);**
Edelmann, Germany (cartons)
Production Manager **Oliver Bedwell**

Client
Kirsty McLeod

Specification
Fedrigoni cartonboard, screenprinting,
blind embossing

This range of off-the-shelf bottles and jars in bespoke cartons was produced for premium skincare specialist Kirsty McLeod. The client's existing identity was a simple 2-color logo: an ornate green frame surrounded the name, printed in black. In order to create maximum standout and a sophisticated and desirable finished product, a very white, embossed board from Fedrigoni was chosen for the carton material. The logo was then screenprinted onto the front, with ingredients and usage printed on the reverse, and a version of the logo blind-embossed on the sides. This created a "chain" effect around the pack and allowed the product to be displayed with alternate print, emboss, print, etc. on the shelf.

Frosted glass jars and bottles maintained
a uniformity across the range, and also
allowed customers a firmer grip when
using the product.

VITRO

Project
Fluted wine bottle/Toccata wine bottle

Clients
Franzia Bros. Winery/Demptos Glass

Specification
Blow-molding, tinting/Tinting

Glass is one of the oldest packaging materials. Its unrivaled qualities of tactility, density, and surface finish make it a preferred choice for high-end products that demand superior finishes, while its inertness also makes it a perfect choice for containing liquids and chemicals. The blow-molding process allows an exceptional range of shapes to be formed in glass. This large-capacity fluted bottle, in glass tinted a light green, appears to stand taller still due to its narrow base and broad shoulders, which give it an angled profile that accentuates its verticality. The Toccata bottle, in antique green glass, has been designed to seal using a standard cork, though different closures can be achieved with modifications to the design of the neck.

VITRO

Project
Vinoseal wine bottle/Classique wine bottle

Design
Art Director/Designer **Efrain Karchmer (Vinoseal bottle)**

Client
Encore Glass/Vitro Stock

Specification
Glass stopper/Blow-molding, tinting

The character of a glass bottle is defined by the mold into which the glass ingot is blown. Surface finish, coloring, and the shape of the body are key attributes that the designer can use to manipulate the user experience when exploiting glass. In the antique-green Vinoseal bottle, slight design modifications to a standard wine bottle have created a finish that is more sophisticated. The slender form, long neck, deep punt, and bespoke closure give this bottle an elegant and refined character. It is cleverly finished through detailing in the neck, which accommodates a glass stopper rather than a standard cork. The shoulder of the Classique bottle has been lowered, giving it an elongated neck and the appearance of a stouter body. The choice of coloring—dead-leaf green—also plays an important role in the way the finish is perceived.

VITRO

Project
**Screw-top, plastic top, and ROPP-closure
wine bottles**

Client
Vitro Stock

Specification
Blow-molding, tinting

The form, color, and surface texture of the
bottle are not the only attributes designers
can manipulate in glass packaging and its
type of finish. There are a number of ways
that different closures can be applied to
a glass bottle, which, in turn, affect the final
appearance. Unlike the common cork closure,
the mold in these designs allows for either
an "antipilfer" screw cap, a plastic cap, or
a resealable aluminum closure to be used.

VITRO/DIAGEO

Project
Embossed flask

Design
Art Director/Designer **Raul Salas Bazaldua**

Client
Diageo

Specification
Embossing, blow-molding

The designer has exploited many of the key attributes of glass to produce a distinctive and customized container evocative of early liquor bottles. The unique shape attracts attention, while the embossed lettering provides an added sensual and visual quality. The natural fluidity of the material, which causes the surface to be irregular rather than perfectly even, has been used to good effect, giving the bottle an antique character and intriguing quality. The method of sealing the bottle is a distinctive plastic-topped cork.

VITRO

Project
Root beer bottle

Client
White Rock

Specification
Vitro cured ink, preprinted tray

A key benefit of glass packaging is that customized designs and branding can be applied to the surface of the bottle rather than being achieved through the design of the bottle itself. This significantly reduces costs while maintaining a high degree of design flexibility and quality. Many brands avoid the high setup costs of manufacturing bespoke molds and instead use standard molds, allowing them to invest in the design and application of labels and inks to the bottle's surface to deliver a strong visual message and reinforce brand imagery.

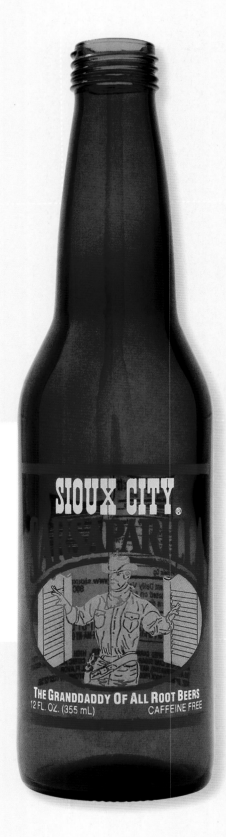

FRUTZZO/VITRO

Project
Juice bottle

Design
**Art Directors/Designers George Xantos/
Raul Salas Bazaldua**

Client
Frutzzo

Specification
Ceramic label, vacuum-sealed cap, transparent glass,
embossing

The transparency of glass is a quality that can
be suppressed through the use of colorants
in the glass. The degree of clarity or opacity
can be precisely what the product demands.
In this instance, where the product is a range
of organic fruit juices, the appetizing, intense,
and alluring colors become an integral part
of the finish. The transparent glass and
ceramic labeling maximize the customer's
view of the product and its enticing qualities.
In addition to the choice of glass, the physical
design of the bottle appeals to the customer's
senses through the sensuous curves of its
ergonomic form and the tactile qualities of
the embossed detailing, most notably the
motif on the neck. The bottle uses a vacuum-
sealed metal cap for a closure.

VITRO

Project
Square bottle with wide opening

Design
Art Directors/Designers **Raul Salas Bazaldua**

Client
Custom Blends

Specification
Square-section bottle

A circular section is that most commonly used for bottles. This can be further adapted by varying the circumference of the section to create gentle contours and a distinctive profile. The production finish in this example adopts a different technique to differentiate the bottle from its competitors by employing a squared section, giving the bottle an idiosyncratic appearance and a solid, bricklike quality. The wide opening makes it easier to manufacture than similar bottles with a narrower neck, as in the latter the contrast between a narrow neck and the square bottle makes the mold more complicated and the package less robust. A wider opening also makes it easier to pour the contents. The choice of a transparent finish was influenced by the nature of the product—in this case organic fruit juices, which flaunt enticing and vibrant natural colors inside the clear package.

VITRO

Project
Standard liquor bottle

Client
Vitro Stock

Specification
Square-section bottle, blow-molding

A square section has been employed in this bottle together with a slight taper, giving the walls of the bottle an angle that helps create an appealing profile and allows the lines of the corners to flow smoothly into the shoulders of the bottle and up to the neck. The molding required to bring these elements together successfully, both aesthetically and structurally, is quite complex. This is a characteristic of the overall production finish, which evokes a sense of quality and eminence befitting a high-end product such as this.

VITRO

Project
Period-design bottle

Design
Art Director/Designer **Raul Salas Bazaldua**

Client
Polar Beverages

Specification
Ceramic label

Glass, unlike plastic and other, more modern materials, has been used for packaging for hundreds of years. This allows designers to come up with designs that replicate antique bottles to evoke a sense of nostalgia. The physical design of this bottle deliberately employs this strategy by reproducing the form and profile of old bottles, while the graphic design augments this theme through the choice of typography and color scheme. The method of applying the graphic information to the bottle, however, is far from antiquated, as it uses ceramic labeling.

VITRO

Project
Cocktail mixer

Design
Art Director/Designer **Raul Salas Bazaldua**

Client
Ryco Packaging

Specification
Blow molding

The specialty-packing industry is big business, and glass allows brands to package their products in high-quality, one-off designs for promotional purposes. This bottle was produced by a leading brand of spirits to contain a limited-edition cocktail mix. The physical design of the bottle takes the cocktail theme to its logical conclusion by creating a cocktail-mixer shape complete with wide-mouthed opening.

PEARLFISHER

Project
Absolut Mandrin bottle

Client
Absolut Vodka

Specification
Frosted glass, colored punt

Glass provides an exceptionally exciting platform on which to apply different printing and production finishes. The design for this world-famous brand exploits the material's credentials fully by offsetting the product's arresting divergent typefaces with the frosted surface finish of the glass, so presenting the customer with an iconic, cool experience. This particular product supplements this theme with an unexpected and witty twist in the base. The colored punt demanded a technical innovation before it could be made commercially viable but, with this achieved, the clever design motif came to represent, physically and graphically, the essence of the product's flavor—inserting the orange "tang" into tangible. When released in the USA, this product became the most successful ever in the Absolut product range.

ABSOLUT®
Country of Sweden
MANDRIN

Absolut Mandrin is made from a unique blend of natural mandarin and orange flavors and vodka distilled from grain grown in the rich fields of southern Sweden. The distilling and flavoring of vodka is an age-old Swedish tradition. Vodka has been sold under the name Absolut since 1879.

40% ALC./VOL. (80 PROOF)   700 ML.
IMPORTED
MANDARIN FLAVORED VODKA
PRODUCED AND BOTTLED IN ÅHUS, SWEDEN
V&S VIN&SPRIT AB (PUBL.)

ABSOLUT MANDRIN

Country of Sweden

Absolut Mandrin is made from a unique blend of natural mandarin and orange flavors and vodka distilled from grain grown in the rich fields of southern Sweden. The distilling and flavoring of vodka is an age-old Swedish tradition. Vodka has been sold under the name Absolut since 1879.

40% ALC./VOL. (80 PROOF) 700 ML.

IMPORTED

MANDARIN FLAVORED VODKA
PRODUCED AND BOTTLED IN ÅHUS, SWEDEN
V&S VIN&SPRIT AB (PUBL)

TURNSTYLE

Project
DRY Soda bottles and pack

Design
Art Director/Designer **Steven Watson**

Client
DRY Soda Company

Specification
Screenprinted label, cartonboard, offset lithography

The brand identity in this range of products has been clearly translated across two different materials and surfaces through the sympathetic use of separate printing techniques. The luscious hues that reflect the flavor and appearance of each product are offset against the liquid in the glass bottles and against the white background of the cartonboard carry cases. The screenprinted labeling on the bottle has been kept to the minimum, maintaining the pure character of the product. This theme is continued throughout the carry case, where typography is applied sparsely and surfaces are bathed in the color that represents the product flavor.

LAVENDER
SODA

KUMQUAT
SODA

The motif of bubbles, composed of five different-sized circles, is a clever and subtle unifying detail repeated across three material finishes: the cartonboard carry case, the glass bottle, and the metal crown cap.

DRY™ SODA: KUMQUAT / 12 FL OZ (35₅
PRODUCED BY:
refreshing citrus. sweet and tart. all na

WEBB SCARLETT deVLAM

Project
Plymouth Gin bottle

Client
V&S Absolut Spirits

Specification
Blow molding, full-color plus metallic spot colors

Radically redesigning the packaging for market-leading brands is a high-risk endeavor. In attempting to expand the boundaries of established markets, efforts to improve the physical and visual character of the brand run the risk of alienating established users and undermining core product values. The redesign of this world-famous brand and distinguished product sought inspiration from the decadent 1920s and 1930s, a period famed for its dancehalls, jazz, and modernity. Oiling society's hedonistic ways was a newfound partiality for cocktails—especially those based on gin, and Plymouth Gin was the brand of choice. The finish of this bottle venerates that era with stunning angular lines that reflect both art-deco style and the smooth-finished purity of a cut-crystal decanter. The hugely successful redesign draws on the authentic heritage of the brand in a style that resonates with a global audience and is perceived as being more high-class. This success prompted the expansion of the range and the design of two further bottles in this brand's portfolio.

The graphics on the label further enhance the bottle's precise character, the angular lines complementing the complex glass surfaces and augmenting the bottle's stately profile.

WEBB SCARLETT deVLAM

Project
Reschke wine bottle, label, and packaging

Design
Art Director/Designer **Edouard Ball and Nicky Kukulka**

Client
Reschke Wines

Specification
VinoLok glass stopper, screenprinting onto glass

Both production and printing finishes have been subtly employed to create a distinguished and highly successful packaging solution that has contributed to exceptional sales and added appeal for a very modest outlay. The design brief demanded a strong image that raised the product above the price wars that occur at the middle and lower end of this market. A key strategy was to employ an alternative means of sealing the bottle, which in turn demanded a different production finish. A VinoLok glass stopper was used that not only elevates the image of the bottle but also encourages its reuse, perhaps as a stylish table-water bottle or olive-oil decanter. This extends the package's life while at the same time delivering lasting brand presence. This is achieved by screen-printing the key brand motifs onto the glass under the impermanent paper label in an etched-glass effect that is subtle, stylish, and conveys eminence. The overall finish is deliberately simple and uncluttered, creating a beautiful and elegant design that does not overstate the brand.

Because the bottle has to be properly sealed, the glass stopper has to be covered, hiding its eminent appearance. A unique neck label was therefore created that highlights the fact that there is a glass stopper on the bottle.

WEBB SCARLETT deVLAM

Project
St. Arnou bottle and packing tube

Design
Art Director/Designers Edouard Ball, Nicky Kukulka, Richard Barkaway, Karl Bakker, Lizzy Fisher

Client
St. Arnou Brewery

Specification
Embossing, foil blocking

Designing a range of packaging devices for an established brand entering a new market sector is an extremely challenging brief. In this case, the brand had an established presence in the draught-beer market but was being placed into the potentially highly lucrative "off-premises" market. Production and printing finishes played a central role in creating a series of packaging devices that reinforced the brand's eminence and established a formidable presence in the upper end of its target market. Designed to stand proud, the shape of the bottle, with its characteristically pinched neckline, forms a recognizable and dependable image of premium quality. The labels have detailed embossing and foiling that further raise the standard of the proprietary bottle. Innovation in the structure and embossing of the six-pack positioned the brand as an unquestionably premium product within its category.

FLIPFLOP DESIGN LTD.

Project
Seisui bottle and box

Design
Art Director/Designer **Lee Saxelby**

Specification
1-color offset printing, 400gsm mirri card, cartonboard

The inspiration for this package, comprising a glass bottle and cartonboard container, was Japanese aesthetics. Though the name provides perhaps the closest connection (Seisui means purity in Japanese), the most conspicuous associations are the floral design, which echoes Japanese blockprints, and, more subtly, the curvature of the glass bottle and its lid, which mimic the outline of a Japanese pagoda. The printing finish on the outer container has been achieved using 1-color process on mirri card. The purple tone was chosen for its suggestion of tranquillity and calmness, while giving the stark white of the floral pattern and product title a beauty in their dignified prominence against the dark background. The same noble appearance is achieved in the glass bottle, which has been tinted purple, with the white floral design and title printed directly onto the glass.

DESIGN BRIDGE

Project
Macallan Whisky bottle

Client
Macallan Whisky

Specification
Molded glass, woodturning

The purity and preeminence of the product is lovingly revered in this design, which uses a number of distinguished finishes to set it apart from potential competitors. This has been achieved through a combination of the physical design, choice of materials and printing finishes. The physical character of the glass bottle is most distinctive, its bulbous, organic form so markedly different from the often formal range of geometric shapes used by similar products in the market. Crowning this curvaceous body is the equally eye-catching feature of the wooden screwcap that has been turned to have a slight swelling and rounded top that matches the shapely nature of the glass bottle beneath. The printed graphics provide the exceptional finishing touches. The textural quality of the leaves' skeletal structure is created by the white print contrasting with the rich tones of the whisky. Furthermore, this design is continued on the back of the bottle, so that from any angle the shadowy motif can be seen through the liquid, giving the whole package a sense of depth and reinforcing the brand's eminent identity.

The graphic design has been kept to a minimum so as not to constrain the leaf motifs, allowing them to appear to dance freely on the surface of the bottle. This has been realized by a careful choice of fonts and their respective positioning in relation to the leaves.

DESIGN BRIDGE

Project
London Dry Gin bottle

Client
Chivas

Specification
Embossing, molded glass

A combination of printing and production finishes has been used on this bottle to create a stately appearance that augments the branding of this renowned product. The rectilinear form of the body, with its high, square shoulders, gives the bottle an upright posture, evocative of the figure in the center of the transparent label. The red screw cap performs a similar role, by echoing the figure's headgear. This majestic red is further used in the branding that appears as an unmistakable header on the label, above the figure but below the bottle's shoulder line. While the visual message is strong and leaves a lasting impression, the consumer experience is further heightened by the bold use of embossing on two of the four sides of the bottle and at the base of the neck. The large fonts offer both a tactile quality when holding the bottle and an evident but subtle visual message suggestive of the quality of the product and its origins.

FLIPFLOP DESIGN LTD.

Project
Senspa bottles

Design
Art Director/Designer **Shayda Azar**

Client
Senspa

Specification
Silkscreen printing, spray painting

This range of products employs similar printing and production finishes across different packaging types to ensure a cohesive and coherent brand identity. The white floral pattern, subtly distinct for each product, appears in an analogous style and type of finish: silkscreen printed onto glass that has been tinted using an ink spray that gives the surface of the glass a textured matte finish. Screenprinting directly onto glass eliminates the need for printed labels and, in this product range, enhances the overall appearance and perceived value of the packaging. The choice of plain white closures helps to maintain the purity and visual simplicity of each container.

The choice of rich earthy colors and the tactility produced by the matte finish are deliberate design choices made to reflect and maintain the brand's natural characteristics.

FLIPFLOP DESIGN LTD.

Project
True Red bottle and box

Design
Art Director/Designer **Lee Saxelby**

Client
Marks & Spencer

Specification
400gsm holographic cartonboard, foil blocking,
2 colors, spray painting, gloss varnish

A scintillating and glamorous appearance has
been achieved in the design of this glass bottle
and its outer packaging. Manufactured from
400gsm red holographic cartonboard, the outer
packaging presents a dazzling effect created
by the board's glitzy finish and the typographic
treatment. The typography is deliberately
minimalist so as not to encroach upon the
necessarily generous areas of holographic
print, but the brand and product names have
been produced using silver foil blocking. This
choice of finish complements the shimmering
appearance of the red background to complete
the overall design. Inside, the curvilinear
profile of the bottle is suggestive of a female
figure, the concave lines of the upper half
terminating at the plastic lid in a manner
evocative of an ostentatious hairdo. The
bottle's slender lines create an attractive
and alluring appearance complemented by
the deep red tones created by the 2 colors
sprayed onto the glass and finished with
a gloss varnish.

FLIPFLOP DESIGN LTD.

Project
Truly Cherish bottle and box

Design
Art Director/Designer Lee Saxelby

Client
Marks & Spencer

Specification
Cartonboard, 2-color offset printing, foil blocking, spray painting

The new range of print finishes employed in this two-part package was part of a rebranding exercise. The personality of the product had to be retained, but its overall appearance improved. This was achieved by maintaining the original two colors and supplementing them with silver foil blocking to display the rose motif, a visually captivating detail that also hints at the fragrance of the product within. A solid frame of black or blue provides a distinctive border around these elements. The elegance of the outer container also performs a marketing role, as it helps to ensure that the packaging will continue to be used throughout the product's life rather than being disposed of after purchase. Inside, the striking jewel-shaped glass bottle has been colored using a semi-transparent blue spray that corresponds with the color schemes on the outer container.

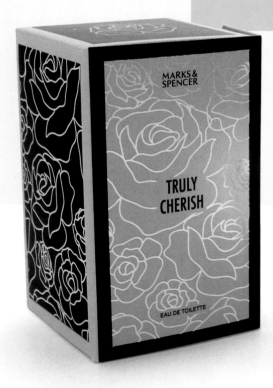

RICE DESIGN

Project
Miniature liquor bottles

Design
Art Director **Takashi Fujita**

Client
Suntory Co. Ltd.

Specification
Metallic adhesive paper label, etched glass,
ROPP screw caps

Distinctive printing finishes have been applied to both the labels and the caps of this range of miniature bottles to create a strong brand image as well as a bold individual appearance in each design. The vivid hues of the central portion of the label, repeated in the text as well as in a metallic finish on the cap, display a bright and refreshing message that is augmented by the icy freshness of the silver printing behind and the frosted glass of the bottle. The names of each product appear in a large typeface printed in white and inlaid in the silver background. The frosted glass is created during the manufacturing process to create a textured finish that is both physically intriguing and visually appealing.

RICE DESIGN

A highly effervescent appearance has been achieved in the physical and graphic design of this range of fruit drinks. The lively, fruity character is heightened by the strong colors, the vibrant nature of the graphic imagery, and the physical form of the bottle. The intense colors of the product provide the foundation of the composition, and the same colors are repeated in the distinguishing features of the label. The energetic design and vivid printing present an eye-catching design that stands out from the competition at the point of sale.

Project
Suntory drinks bottles

Design
Art Director **Takashi Fujita**

Client
Suntory Co. Ltd.

Specification
Metallic adhesive paper label, ROPP screw caps

Production finishes augment the distinctive graphic imagery of the label by creating the idiosyncratic shape of the bottle. The broad and slightly bulbous form presents an image suggestive of fun and enjoyment.

MAJESTIC METAL

Innovations in production processes have brought metal packaging a long way since the first days of the tinplate can in the early 19th century. Even then, the discovery of tinplating iron as a means of protecting food containers was a major advance that revolutionized metal packaging and changed the industry forever. Today metal packaging is a multitrillion-dollar business, delivering an almost infinite range of design solutions to the packaging industry. Enhanced manufacturing and materials processes and improved design insure that metal maintains its position as one of the leading materials available to the packaging industry. These continual improvements have allowed metal containers to be forged into amazing shapes, to be sealed with an array of closures, and to lessen their impact on the environment through lightweighting and improved recyclability.

CROWN SPECIALITY PACKAGING

Project
Altoids dispenser

Client
Callard & Bowser

Specification
Debossing, embossing

The exceptional physical properties of metal have been exploited innovatively to create a mechanical two-piece resealable container. Unlike many metal containers that rely on the customary detachable lid and base, the two components of this package are not detachable and slide apart, though not completely, to dispense the product. The process of opening and closing the package provides a tactile experience that is enhanced and assisted by the attention to detail in its design. The rounded lip of the base and the lightly raised curved surface of the lid into which mild debossing and embossing has been applied help augment the printed graphics. When closed, the package is an impressive standalone container, fitting comfortably in the palm of the hand, purse or pocket, making it a desirable device and adding value to the product.

CROWN SPECIALITY PACKAGING

Project
Iced Tea can

Client
Teisseire

Specification
Tinplate can, UV printing, soft-touch varnish

Developments in production techniques for beverage cans have improved significantly since the early days of simple rolling and pressing. Today, sophisticated forms and shapes can be mass-produced to create very strong product imagery and reinforce brand identity. Here, subtle curves and gentle contours generate a vessel that is both ergonomically satisfying as well as visually pleasing. While these effects are successful in terms of their physical attributes, they present challenges for the printing industry: it has to keep pace with such manufacturing advances by delivering high-quality printed finishes that do not distort when applied over graduations in the surface of the package.

A "soft-touch" varnish has been used to augment the package's tactility and further improve the overall sensuous experience.

DAVIES LESLIE-SMITH

Project
Buzz Off spray cans

Design
Art Director/Designer **Tim Leslie-Smith**

Client
Superdrug

Specification
Aluminum spray cans, 5 colors, matte finish

Printing and production finishes can be used very effectively to unite a range of products under a single brand image. In this series of products, a matte finish over the minimalist and fresh design set against a black background printed using a 5-color process produces a consistent appearance for the product range. Individual product types are distinguished most conspicuously through the color of the lid. Each color reflects the character of the product, while the semi-transparent quality maintains the brand identity and differentiates it from competitors at the point of sale. The choice of aluminum as the principal packaging material gives each container a solid and cool character consistent with the objectives of the printed design.

FLIPFLOP DESIGN LTD.

Project
Travel toiletries sachets

Design
Art Director/Designer **Lee Saxelby**

Client
Marks & Spencer

Specification
Aluminum foil sachets, offset/flexographic printing

Packaging materials often have exceptional finishes in their own right and therefore can be used to augment alternative applied finishes. This range of products demonstrates the effective and impressive complementary use of the packaging material and a printing finish to create a charismatic appearance for an entire brand. Aluminum foil provides the base for each of the packages; its satin, light gray sheen projects a clinical, crisp, and superior tone that contrasts strongly and deliberately with the vivid colors of the photographic images. The high-quality reproduction of these images is essential to the effective outcome of the overall design. Each image has been carefully selected to reflect the nature of the product so that consumers can guess the contents of each sachet from the photograph through the associations it evokes.

The use of the printed photographic image as a means of creating the bold typography down the left of each package is a conspicuous detail that helps to reinforce both the product and the brand's distinguished imagery. It also serves the functional task of displaying information.

CROWN SPECIALITY PACKAGING

Project
Two-piece tub prototype

Client
Self-initiated

Specification
Tinplate can, soft-touch varnish, embossing

Tactility is one of many sensuous experiences that the use of varnishes, printing techniques, and manufacturing processes can deliver effectively to alter the physical impression of the package with relative ease. A "soft-touch" varnish has been applied to this two-part steel tub, giving it a tactile quality that enhances the user experience. Furthermore, the embossed motifs in bright colors against a black background beneath the coat of varnish adds to the visual and physical quality of the package.

Embossing and, conversely, debossing work best and create their greatest impact when applied to broad, unadorned surfaces. This heightens the contrast, either visually or physically, between different surfaces and reinforces the surface detailing.

CROWN SPECIALITY PACKAGING

Project
Perforated can prototype

Client
Self-initiated

Specification
Tinplate can, perforation

Other than the use of inks and varnishes, or employing manufacturing techniques that alter a package's shape, an alternative way to exploit the visual and tactile quality of a metal package is to change its finished surface. Familiar techniques are embossing and debossing, but less common is the use of perforation. This is partly because it can reduce the protective qualities of the package, making this technique unusable for some products, but perforation can none the less be used as an eye-catching device that is open to extensive creative opportunities.

The perforations in this example have been applied in a regular size and shape to demonstrate the technique, but different sizes, shapes, and patterns of perforation could also be used to improve the overall effect.

LGMT 3/1
General purpose
SKF Bearing grease
Graisse Fett Grasa
Grasso شحم الكريات الكرية

SKF

CROWN SPECIALITY PACKAGING

Project
Holographic tin

Client
SKF

Specification
Tinplate can, holographic printing

Holographic printing delivers an unmistakable effect. Its conspicuous characteristics are commonly exploited by the packaging industry to grab attention and, sometimes, add value. However, this jazzy quality does not always need to be used for its appearance alone. It is perhaps surprising to find it under the base of a tin of something as unglamorous as bearing grease, but this intelligent design uses the distinctive qualities of holography to insure product authenticity. Counterfeiting is a major problem in some industries—especially where substandard products can compromise safety, as here with automotive components—so the holographic finish to this can is therefore a seal of authenticity, its unique characteristics reassuring rather than dazzling the user.

CROWN FOOD EUROPE

The application of a simple manufacturing process has transformed a regular metal can into something tangibly distinct from its competitors. Both production and printing techniques have been used here to create an idiosyncratic and physically appealing metal can with a memorable finish, as the vertical columns created during the manufacturing process physically enhance the surface finish.

Project
Fluted can

Client
Stockmeyer

Specification
Contoured tinplate can, 4-color process

The application of printed graphics has been carefully considered to accentuate the varying contours of the package's surface by displaying the ingredients of the product within each column, suggestive of fresh ingredients falling into a cooking pot, while also giving the upper part of the package a dignified upright appearance.

ASA SAN MARINO

Project
Colombo Oil two-part package

Client
Various

Specification
UV-printing, tinplate, cardboard, die-cutting

Different materials used together in primary, secondary, and sometimes tertiary packaging can create a memorable effect that enhances the presentation of the overall package. This approach is frequently used with high-end products, where the added outlay in extra packaging materials can be borne by the relatively high price of the product. However, this need not be confined only to the most exclusive product ranges. Through clever design, different materials, production techniques, and printing can be combined in efficient and highly effective ways. In this example, the packaging for olive oil includes a cartonboard outer container that has been die-cut to accommodate the shaped steel bottle securely. The refreshing design has been effectively applied to both surfaces, so that when combined they blend into one another and appear to be one. This effect is complicated by having to print on the curves of the metal container without distortion, which would become more apparent against the flat surface of the cartonboard outer package.

www.gruppoasa.com

COLOMBO
Customized Olive Oil Metallic Bottle

Todas las virtudes

del metal para contener

y preservar de la mejor

manera posible

tu producto

Ceci n'est pas une bouteille.

GRUPPO ASA

COLOMBO

GRUPPO ASA

Different materials reproduce inks in very different ways, so the continuity of the graphic image across cartonboard and metal when both components of the packaging are united requires careful consideration. The die-cut also plays an important role both in securing the bottle while in transit as well as at the point of sale, and it reinforces the continuity of the pattern by holding the bottle in place.

PEARLFISHER

Project
Nude cosmetics tubs and tubes

Client
Nude

Specification
Bespoke Pantone inks, biodegradable sleeve

It is not uncommon in packaging design for less to mean very much more, and this range of packaging exemplifies this view. It was created as part of the generation of a brand identity—including logotype, packaging, and web design—for a new ecofriendly range of skincare products. The principle behind the product range is that whatever we put on our skin is as important as what we put in our mouths. Consequently, the products are 100 percent natural, organic where possible, and free from parabens, sulfates, and other chemical nasties. The packaging design is the logical conclusion of this principle, communicating simplicity and purity with a pared-down, minimal look and feel, using a bespoke Pantone color palette created specially for this brand with muted tones, and earthy feel to imitate the shades of nature. The package's physical structure augments this natural theme with simple ergonomic curves and smooth finishes inspired by pebbles.

All mandatory information has been printed on a removable and completely biodegradable sleeve that can be discarded to leave the packaging—aptly—naked.

DECANOVA

Project
Diamond box

Client
Tsarina Diamond

Specification
Steel packaging, die-cut plastic window, velvet lining, foam insert

Some products demand exceptional packaging. In such cases the designer is required to consider a redefinition of the usual parameters with materials, finishes, and production techniques. Few products can mean more to the consumer than a diamond ring, and in this example the inimitable product has received a fittingly inimitable packaging solution that has reconsidered the standard brief and dispensed with the customary hinged box and fabric inlay. Instead, a refreshing and innovative answer has been sought that uses a round metal tin with a transparent plastic window through which the product is instantly visible. The box is constructed in two parts. The base contains a velvet-covered foam insert that clasps the partially submerged ring; the lid contains a round central window that allows the ring to be framed while also providing a suitable platform on which printed graphics and product branding can be applied.

The manufacture of the lid required particular consideration to allow the window to be fixed without the need for unsightly adhesive or finishes, so leaving the package clean, crisp, and immediately desirable.

GLUD & MARSTRAND

Project
Lakritsi tin

Client
Oy Halva Ab

Specification
Black ink veneer, stamping

On this package, a veneer of soft black ink on metal provides the foundation for a lucid appearance that boasts exceptional clarity of printed graphics. The choice of printing finish and the shape of the container have been chosen to intimate the product contained within, and, in so doing, produce a tactile effect and an almost edible evocation of the silky surface finish of liquorice. With such a bold black background there is no need for subtle hints and gradients in the printing, which would only detract from the eminent simplicity of the overall concept. Instead, all fonts and graphics are boldly stamped onto the surface in just two colors plus white to create a dramatic illustration that upholds the exclusiveness of a product targeted at the discerning customer. The material and its untainted surface texture are essential to the success of the whole composition, visually and tactilely, as well as to the phenomenal success in the marketplace in which it experienced a threefold increase in sales since the redesign.

The decision to replace previous foil-bag packaging with a metal tin was one not only aimed at making a statement about exclusivity in a highly competitive market but was also a marketing decision that acknowledged the fact that users would keep the package and that its reuse would serve as a marketing device long after its contents had been consumed.

BOXAL

Project
Desperados bottles

Client
Brasserie Fischer

Specification
6-color dry offset, brushed aluminum substrate, gloss varnish

Only a few years ago, bottles used for the commercial packaging of liquids were almost always made from glass or, occasionally, ceramics. This established status quo has been radically shaken since the advent of the metal bottle. Elaborately shaped aluminum bottles were previously unthinkable, but with advances in manufacturing technologies it is not only possible to manufacture bottles from a single piece, it is also cheap. This atypical packaging medium—so easily distinguishable from its main competitor, glass—offers customers a unique experience through the material's characteristic qualities, which, in turn, helps to boost brand recognition. Metal packaging is also a versatile medium on which to apply printed graphics, thereby further enhancing the package's already excellent characteristics. Here, three different designs for a range of drinks demonstrate the extremely high-definition print finish, using a 6-color process, that can be applied to the surface of metal bottles. The same level of detail is not possible on the surface of glass, other than by using shrink sleeves or labels.

GLUD & MARSTRAND

Project
Peel off lid

Client
Self-initiated

Specification
Peel-off metal lid, embossing

Technological innovations in printing and production are constantly pushing the boundaries of design. This assists designers as much as it challenges them, presenting new opportunities and opening up previously unexplored areas of practice. The peel-off lid radically changed the means by which metal packaging can be opened, thus improving the consumer's experience and making the task much easier than traditional metal packaging, which requires a mechanical device to gain access to the product. While the increased efficiency of this design serves an important functional role, it also offers an entirely new field of exploration for designers applying printing and production finishes on and around the lid of metal packaging. The appearance of the peel-off lid is conspicuous in its distinction from other metal packs on the market, and it evokes a physical finish that is very modern —a characteristic that in many applications might be very desirable.

GLUD & MARSTRAND

Project
Celebration package

Client
Tulip, in cooperation with Nongshim

Specification
Tinplate, full-color plus metallic gold

In this example, two different types of packaging have been incorporated into a single large container to create a specialty package to celebrate the bicentenary of Hans Christian Andersen's birth. Though it is a Danish product, the packaging has been designed specifically for the Korean market, in which culture the giving of gifts plays a significant role, both privately and for business, especially during national and cultural festivals. The distinctive gleaming golden finish provides an appealing foundation on the outer container, with photographs of Hans Christian Andersen and graphic motifs and original sketches depicting scenes from his stories. The sense of history engendered by this imagery and printing style augments the assuredness and exclusivity of the material, which replaced the cardboard used for previous designs for this product. The decisions taken regarding design and print proved decisive in the exceptional success of the gift box, which contains four metal containers of premium-quality ham. The composition of the whole package evokes a sense of traditional values, as befits a trusted and reputable product through its association with a world-famous children's author. The prominent appearance and robust materials of the outer container make it both a desirable and a functional product, long after the ham inside has been consumed. The two different sizes of packaging display almost identical printed finishes, comprising solid blocks of color, strong graphic fonts, and photographic representations of the product along with its distinctive ingredients. The use of bold colors behind the text and product imagery serves to unite the elements of the graphic design into a cohesive and intelligible whole.

BOXAL

Project
Burn bottle

Client
Coca-Cola

Specification
6-color dry offset, brushed aluminum substrate, gloss varnish

Different finishing techniques help to make the appearance of this aluminum bottle instantly recognizable. The coat of black that shrouds the entire body, from the top of the neck to the base, has been cleverly differentiated by utilizing the necking and shaping processes, which produce both gloss and matte finishes—the body of the bottle is stylishly glossy, in contrast with the matte effect around the neck. This contrast is not only visually striking, it also offers the user an interesting tactile experience. Arresting graphics have been used in the form of a flame to complement the themes of the brand, the fiery red-and-yellow hues of the motif, produced using a 6-color process, contrast energetically with the dominant black background.

BOXAL

Project
Coca-Cola Christmas bottle

Client
Coca-Cola

Specification
6-color dry offset, brushed aluminum substrate,
gloss varnish

The advent of metal-bottle packaging has heralded rapid advances in printing techniques that can apply high-definition graphics onto a bottle without any distortion being caused by the varying contours on the surface. This complex process is achieved by printing directly onto the straight-walled aluminum surface using pre-distortion techniques so that, when the bottle is shaped, the final printed finish appears undistorted. Few bottles have such instantly recognizable contours as that of Coca-Cola, the shapely form of which was created many decades ago. Transferring this key facet of the brand's identity to an aluminum bottle was, doubtless, a challenge, but it has enabled a veritable revolution in the level of detail that can be applied to the container. Illustrated here is a limited-edition version, which demonstrates the exceptional finish that can be applied to aluminum-bottle packaging, both in the level of detail that can be printed as well as the range of colors.

BOXAL

Project
Coca-Cola BlaK bottle

Client
Coca-Cola

Specification
6-color dry offset, brushed aluminum substrate,
gloss varnish

While the distinctively curvaceous form
of this brand might have been successfully
reproduced in aluminum, it is the printing
finish that arrests the viewer's attention in
this design. The gloss-black base, which
fades to matte as it nears the neck, provides
a stylish platform on which the gold-and-
white typefaces and graphics stand out
stunningly. This effect has been achieved
using pre-distortion printing techniques as
well as by taking advantage of the natural
finishes that result from the necking and
shaping processes that produce the matte
and gloss finishes. Subtler graphic devices
accentuate the bottle's shapely form, including
the gold streak extending the height of the
bottle, and the darker red tones in which can
be seen illustrations of carbonated bubbles,
so giving the illusion of transparency.

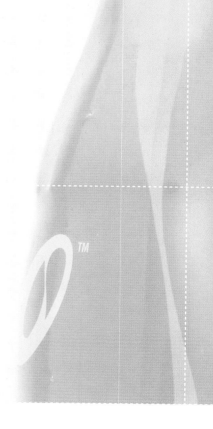

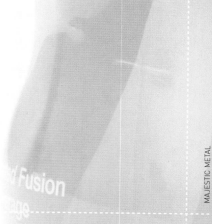

BOXAL

Project
MP3 deodorant can range

Client
Self-initiated

Specification
6-color dry offset, brushed aluminum substrate,
matte over varnish

In this example, production and printing
techniques have been used to create a finish
that incorporates subtle design details that
perform functional as well as aesthetic roles.
Here, the raised nodules in the smooth metal
surface of the aerosol provide a tactile element
that attracts the attention and almost demands
that the can be grasped. This combined visual
and tactile role improves the user experience
by enhancing grip and control when applying
the product. The printed finish highlights
these manufacturing details by contrasting
the bare aluminum surface with the printed
ellipses that cover the surface on and around
the small protuberances.

PIRLO

Project
ColorEye paint tin

Client
Self-initiated

Specification
Tin, polypropylene window, injection molding

Metal is the staple packaging material for the paint industry because of its excellent strength and its protective qualities which insure the secure and safe containment of chemicals. However, its principal disadvantage is that it cannot satisfy the very specific demand for accurate color rendition. This has traditionally been achieved by the costly and labor-intensive application of labels and color swatches to the can. With new, relatively simple technological developments it is now possible to insert a plastic window in the lid of the paint can. This means that not only can the exact color of the paint be seen but users can also judge for themselves the viscosity of the paint. Branded the ColorEye, this has reduced costs and improved packaging performance. The plastic used is a particular type of polypropylene that offers a high degree of transparency as well as being able to withstand contact with the chemicals in the paint and be tough enough to be fully stackable during transportation and at the point of sale. The windows are injection molded and then inserted into the lid with a permanent seal between the plastic and the metal that guarantees the physical integrity of the package.

WEBB SCARLETT deVLAM

Project
Boss Skin range

Client
Procter & Gamble

Specification
Brushed steel, debossing, twist closure

Designed for brand entry into the highly competitive men's skincare arena, the distinguished packaging finish for this range of products draws inspiration from the qualities and refined purity of German automotive engineering—the precision and raw beauty of machined engine components. Emulating these characteristics in the design of this range went beyond the meticulous use of sleek materials and textured finishes, as the functionality and performance of this unapologetically masculine packaging was also critical to its endorsement and ultimate success. The combination of finishes in this specially designed iconic hero pack confidently communicate these brand values. The range comprises a number of vital characteristics that collectively create a clean, dependable, solid appearance—shape, color, and texture fusing with cool, gray-blue, brushed steel.

For a range of packages that were specifically designed to perform, the caps received special attention to detail, as it was noted that men object to fiddly closures. In respect to the solid and masculine theme employed throughout the packaging range, the self-contained and lockable closures were designed to be integral to the pack, requiring only a simple twist to open and close.

The other necessary graphic content has been applied in a single tone of metallic silver so as not to detract attention from the flame. The use of plain silver on black helps the vibrant red tones to leap visually from the surface of the can.

TOYO SEIKAN

Project
Kirin Fire bottle

Client
Kirin

Specification
Embossing, metallic ink

Printing and production techniques have been combined in this steel drinks can to produce an exceptional visual effect that also boasts a subtle, tactile quality, thus giving the container added appeal. The striking appearance is achieved through the treatment of the flame motif in the center of the can, which also figuratively represents the brand name. The outlines of the flame have been embossed into the walls of the container, drawing attention to its appealingly curvaceous form in a way that suggests that it is flickering. To enhance this visual device, a graduated metallic printing finish has been applied to the voids that make up the flame, which contrasts sharply with the solid-black background. The choice of metallic print gives the red and orange hues a vivacity befitting the character of the flame.

CROWN HOLDINGS, INC.

Project
Altoids tin

Client
Callard & Bowser

Specification
Embossing

Metal packaging possesses a quality that can be hard to match using other packaging materials. Not only can it be forged during the production process to create all manner of appealing shapes, but the quality of its surface makes it an exceptional platform on which to display product information attractively. This world-famous brand uses the material properties of metal to create a physically and visually striking container. The two-part container is largely unadorned on the base, but the lid has been shaped to present a surface on which the product title and brand information is charmingly presented through a combination of production and printing finishes. Embossing has been used to help the brand name stand out from the surface of the container both figuratively and actually, augmented by the choice of printing that appears in a circle on the surface of the lid. It has been left bare over the embossing so that the sheen of the metal surface is used to highlight this particular facet of the package.

The characteristics of the material have been used to create the opening device for the package, which requires the application of pressure to lever the lid from the base. The functional role of this device has been visually marked in the physical form of the package, with the simple instruction "Press" embossed into the surface of the lid.

CROWN FOOD EUROPE

Project
Waistline Baked Beans can

Client
Waistline

Specification
Ribbed metal can, full-color printing

The physical attributes of metal make it a very versatile and desirable packaging material. As well as being 100 percent recyclable and boasting an exceptional surface finish, it can be manufactured in a wide range of different forms and still retain the necessary structural integrity to perform its function. This attribute has been very skillfully utilized in this package design that is visually very distinctive as well as reflecting the brand's purpose. As part of a range of foods aimed at the health- and diet-conscious, the sides of this can have been shaped into a concave profile, evocative of a taut waistline. In the center of the can a series of parallel ribs in the metal provide strength at the weakest point of the structure while also giving a further tactile dimension to the curvaceous body.

CROWN FOOD EUROPE

Project
Stockmeyer Chunky range cans

Client
Stockmeyer

Specification
Contoured metal can, full-color printing

Just as the qualities of metal can be used to create abstract and distinctive shapes, they can also reinforce the brand message. The portly character of this package is strongly suggestive of the product, both in its title as well as its context. The chunkiness of the ingredients is evoked in the equally stocky shape of the can, but the graphics suggest something else—the cooking pot. The solid-black background creates an image that calls to mind the bulky cooking pots of old, a symbol also suggestive of quality ingredients and good, honest cooking.

When using different types of production finishes in the design of uniquely shaped packages it is important to consider the printing finish and how this will be affected by the physical form. If it is not well considered, the contours of a shaped body can just as easily augment the graphic design as it can undermine it. Here, the product information is accentuated on the bulge of the can, giving it added prominence and a sense of shapeliness.

REXAM

Project
Two-piece aluminum squat can

Client
Self-initiated

Specification
Black plus 1 spot color, plastic cap

The range of shapes and capacities of metal consumer packaging has diversified greatly in recent years. Improved production techniques have allowed designers to be more adventurous with their designs while keeping costs relatively low. This design has a similar circumference to standard metal drinks containers but has been reduced in height, which helps distinguish it from competitors at the point of sale, as does the uncommon design feature of a resealable plastic lid. The printing finish draws on the characteristic quality of steel packaging by using the gray metallic sheen as a backdrop to the text and branding, which stands out clearly against it in bright orange and black.

MINERALSALT
MINERALMIX SOM
ERSÄTTER VANLIGT SALT
100% SMAK - BARA 33% VANLIGT SALT

ETT FRÄSCHARE OCH LÄTTARE SALT FÖR DIG SOM
GILLAR GOD MAT OCH ÄR RÄDD OM DIN HÄLSA

REXAM

Project
Two-piece aluminum slim can

Client
Self-initiated

Specification
Aluminum, matte varnish, black plus 1 spot color

The slimline drinks container has become a popular alternative to the larger-diameter containers that once dominated the market. These slender cans are particularly popular in the nonalcoholic drinks market and have experienced considerable growth in the energy-drinks market. The example here demonstrates the necessary considerations for designing printed graphics on this size of container, as, compared with wider cans, printed material has a narrower platform from which to present its message. Here, this has been taken into account by the choice of font and the simplicity of the central circular spiraling motif printed in a vibrant contrast of black and orange. These two elements display all the branding while the necessary descriptive information is printed in a smaller typeface at the base of the container. The background has been left bare to display the qualities of the aluminum surface. A varnish, applied to the entire surface for aesthetic reasons, also protects it from damage and wear that might occur during transportation or at the point of sale.

TOYO SEIKAN

Project
Kirin Fire bottle

Client
Kirin

Specification
Metallic gold ink, ridged steel

Innovations in surface treatments for metal packaging constantly invigorate the market, as one successful application is superseded by another. An exceptional use of surface treatments has been applied to this can in a series of triangular patterns that create a striking structural grid across the central portion of the can. The series of patterns produces a tactile quality that is physically appealing as well as being visually intriguing, as the wide range of different angles in the surface brings out a variety of highlights and shadows. This physical quality augments the printing finish, as diverse shades are created simply by the nature of the container's surface. This is accentuated by the choice of metallic-gold finish, which is particularly effervescent in the way it plays off the uneven surface.

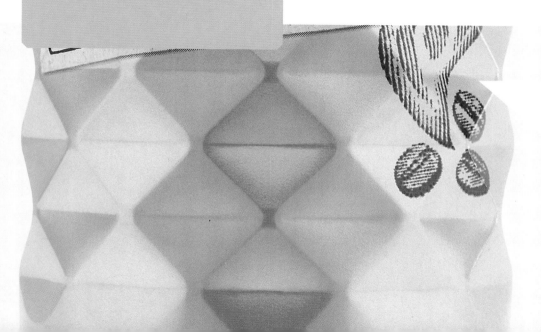

The integrity of the structure of a cylindrical container is an essential consideration when designing production finishes for this type of application. The size of the triangles in this design and the manner in which they encircle the container after it has been folded from a flat sheet insure that the end product is structurally sound and the pattern is not compromised.

REXAM

Project
Two-piece aluminum can

Client
Self-initiated

Specification
360° debossed aluminum, transparent gold coating

High-volume consumer products often rely on generic containers to keep manufacturing and tooling costs down. In such cases, the structural characteristics of the product are subordinate to the printing in conveying an appropriate brand message and distinguishing the product from competitors. This standard-volume beverage can for alcoholic drinks has cleverly bucked this trend by applying vertical ribs to the surface of the container in order to give it a distinctive appearance and a unique tactile quality. The slender, undulating lines interplay teasingly with the printed graphics, giving the container's surface a distinctively furrowed finish. This debossing provides not only a distinguished appearance but also a functional role, as the ribs make the can easier to grip.

Design details pressed into sheet metal before rolling should account for the manufacturing process. Designs should be shallow and relatively small and applied in a vertical orientation, as horizontal details will prevent the sheet from being rolled into a cylinder.

REXAM

Project
Ritmix can

Design
Art Director/Designer **Lee Saxelby**

Client
Ritmix

Specification
Tactile varnish, full-color printing

Varnishing provides a cost-effective way of giving the surface of a package a distinctive finish and a distinguished physical appearance. Whereas production finishes can require additional tooling and longer production times—thereby increasing costs—varnishes are applied after the printing process to give a package physical and visual distinction. This package has had a tactile varnish applied to it that produces a slightly mottled appearance and a skinlike texture. Varnishes are a valuable tool for packaging designers: they are not only capable of providing a wide range of different textures, but they also help protect the integrity of the printing finish, shielding it from abrasion and scratching as well as sealing the printed information and protecting it.

TOYO SEIKAN

Project
Kirin Fire bottle

Client
Kirin

Specification
Varnish, textured finish, steel

The creation of physical and visual attributes
on metal packaging can be achieved not only
through the combination of printing and
production finishes but also, more simply,
through the choice of printing finishes only.
Unlike the other prominent products in its
brand range, this package is distinguished by
a pearlescent appearance. This is created
by the printing and varnishing that leaves the
surface of the container with a lightly textured
feel that is demonstrated also in the way in
which light reflects off the surface of the can.
Unlike most cans, which use gloss printing
and varnishing to give a smooth and shiny
appearance, this package differentiates itself
from potential competitors through its coarse
tactility. The sparkling silver background
provides a solid and appealing foundation for
the main graphic content, which is arranged
on a beige background suggestive of a printed
label. The black text and bold lettering contrast
with the otherwise light treatment to project
the brand name and the product powerfully.

GLUD & MARSTRAND

Project
Caprimo Coffee tin

Client
Barry Callebaut

Specification
4-color process

The reassuring comfort of the product is strongly portrayed by the warm tones of the exceptionally high-quality printing finish on this container. The high-definition full-color printing displays clearly the intricate details of the gold mug and saucer and their inviting, steaming contents. A narrow vertical band of black provides a platform on which the brand logo can be presented clearly along with other suggestive motifs and texts in an elaborate font. While the printing finish is highly influential in establishing the identity and eminence of this product, it is a minor manufacturing detail that provides arguably the strongest visual statement. The gently rounded and slightly bulbous lip of the lid is a design detail that finishes the package in an eminently refined and orderly manner. The printed finish of solid black draws attention to the rounded rim through the strong highlights created on its curved outline. The choice of materials and the container's overall elegance increases the likelihood that consumers will keep the package, and so it will continue to perform a promotional role for the brand.

The solid-black lid presents an effective foundation for displaying the printed logo, itself composed of yellows and blacks. This insures that consumers can identify the package from above if too densely stacked at the point of sale.

GLUD & MARSTRAND

Project
Fox's Creations tin

Client
Fox's Biscuits

Specification
Embossing, paper label

Competition within this market area is intense between a select few prominent brands, and in such an aggressive environment packaging plays a critical role in achieving success and maintaining customer loyalty. The aim of the redesign of the packaging for this popular product was to strengthen and revitalize the brand, and it accomplished these objectives— despite the product and target group remaining unchanged. Where the previous packaging comprised a regular square tin finished with printed graphics, the new design incorporates innovative production finishes that significantly alter its form with a radical printing finish that invigorates the overall appearance. Physically, the package is almost square, but an important distinction has been incorporated into the design by providing large radiuses to two opposite corners. This subtle but significant detail physically distinguishes the container from competitors at the point of sale, while embossing on the lid and the vibrant colors printed onto the metal and throughout the paper labeling augment the package's appeal.

A number of production and printing finishes have been skillfully used to create a cohesive and successful design. The rounded corners give the container an asymmetrical form, which is unusual and distinctive in this product range, but equally gives the container a soft and supple feel that is accentuated by the velvety effect of the printing and the rounded curves of the embossed edges.

GLUD & MARSTRAND

Project
Can2Can cans

Client
Self-initiated

Specification
Plastic ring, steel, spot colors

Innovation is often the key to opening up entirely new fields of packaging opportunities. The design of a simple plastic ring that can be affixed to the top or bottom of a standard-diameter metal can allows these packages to be stacked securely one on top of the other either selectively by the consumer at the point of sale or by the supplier. While grouping cans side-by-side is an established practice, doing it vertically is new and presents a unique and distinctive appearance that suits a wide range of specialty products. Some examples of possible uses include: ready meals, where ingredients might be contained in separate cans; children's party packs, where toys and sweets can be made available in different cans; or coffee, where a range of different coffees might be sold as a gift pack.

This innovation has opened the door wide open to an almost infinite range of production finishes that would suit stacked cans. This example demonstrates the shapely forms of bulbous cans aligned vertically to create a curious and appealing shape that, in metal packaging, has not previously been possible.

The success of this design relies on a
sound understanding of the capabilities of
both the material and the available printing
finishes. The bulbous form enhances the
printed effect of the liquid, which appears
to physically bounce off the side of the
container. Without this physical cue, the
printing, despite its exceptional quality,
would not have the same effect.

GLUD &
MARSTRAND

Project
Milk powder tin

Client
Self-initiated

Specification
Lacquer finish, contoured metal can

As a packaging material, metal has a number
of outstanding qualities that cannot be
achieved with other materials. The physical
characteristics of this container for milk
powder are evidently eye-catching, which, as
a production finish in its own right, is highly
appealing, but, combined with the exceptional
printing finishes, the overall appearance is
a very high-quality packaging solution. The
3-D effect is created by the printing finish,
which reproduces the photograph in high
definition and uses lacquer effects, as well
as the distinctive quality of bare metal at the
top of the container. The interplay between
these elements creates an arresting illusion
and a lively picture that helps present a stronger
brand message. The effect would not be
possible using any other packaging material.

HELVETICA

Project
Holistic Beau-Tea sachet

Client
Natural House

Specification
Matte paper, matte seal, metal foil, adhesive label

Minimalism and freshness are the corner-stones of this packaging for a tea aimed at the natural-food market. The packaging finishes aim to reflect the distinctive characteristics of Japanese culture, both in their appearance and in their physical qualities. The thick foil bag presents a distinctive and eye-catching appearance while also evoking a sense of hygiene and product freshness. Product information and branding are displayed on a simple adhesive label printed in organic tones that depicts the natural qualities of the product. Innovations in production techniques have allowed the bag to be resealable using a zipper along the length of the top, which helps keep the product fresh.

The unadorned and silky texture of the foil bag uses the unique characteristics of metal to provide a tactile finish suggestive of hygiene and quality.

TAB

タブを手前におこし、右に引っぱって下さい。

ZIPPER

HOLISTIC BEAU-TEA　　Oregon Tilth 認証ハーブ100％使用

Natural House

ハーバリストが厳選した7種のハーブのブレンドティ
Reset Blend
リセットブレンド

7包入

HELVETICA

Project
Shiseido vitamin supplement tin and box

Client
Shiseido

Specification
Matte-coated corrugated paper, matte varnish,
matte hot stamp

Shiseido, one of Japan's leading brands of beauty products, started out as a diminutive drugstore that aimed to bring consumers all the benefits of health and beauty products under a single roof. The printing and production finishes used by the brand across its product range are revered by many for their simplicity and purity. This design for the packaging of vitamin supplements maintains this concept while inducing, by using a traditionally styled metal container, a sense of the brand's roots and its proud history. The pack comprises two functional elements: the outer cartonboard container and the inner metal case. A paper pamphlet containing the product instructions sits discreetly beneath the metal container. The outer box is printed in two colors, the predominant effect being created by the soft tones used as a foundation, with a darker ink employed to depict the product crest in the center of the top of the container. A small amount of text appears in white along the front face of the container. Inside, the metal case containing the product has been left unprinted, using the production finish to present the necessary brand message. This is delivered by embossing the circular crest onto the top of the lid to create an undeniably attractive and distinguished appearance. A small adhesive strip, printed in mauve with white lettering, acts as a seal to insure the product's integrity.

The product's distinctive crest has been reproduced through printing on one container and production finishes on the other, creating a strong brand message throughout the whole package at point of sale as well as during and after the product's use.

PIRLO

Project
Braille packaging

Client
Self-initiated

Specification
Tin, embossing

The manufacturing process of applying raised or sunken details in the surface of a package is usually achieved by embossing or debossing. These effects invariably draw attention to certain physical or graphic details and enhance the user experience. However, it is no secret that the aim of employing these techniques is largely aesthetic rather than functional. One reason for using such techniques that rises above mere added value is in the production of Braille for the benefit of visually impaired users. This is a relatively simple process, whether the package's surface is plastic, metal, or cartonboard. In an industry where so much emphasis is placed on appearance, this group is often ignored by designers— but it is essential that designers consider all potential user groups.

WACKY PLASTIC

Of the many different types of packaging materials, plastic is the most recent and most diverse. Because there are so many types, the material boasts an amazing variety of qualities that suit all manner of functions. From rigid receptacles to flexible film, and from transparent trays to kitschy cartons, plastic can satisfy almost every packaging situation. Plastic's exceptional chemical properties and flexibility make it ideal for taking on outlandish colors and being formed into wacky shapes through a wide range of processes, including blowing, vacuum forming, extrusion, and injection blow molding. Plastic is also a very light material, which helps to lessen its impact on the environment during transportation, storage, and disposal, and, in recent years, increasingly efficient recycling processes have helped further improve its environmental credentials.

IF THIS BAG IS FOUND FLOATING IN ANY BODY OF WATER, IT IS BECAUSE THE OWNER NEVER READ THE CONTENTS AND THUS MAY BE PRESUMED DROWNED.

DAVIES LESLIE-SMITH

Project
Darling Spuds packets

Design
Art Director/Designer Steve Davies

Client
Salty Dog Brands

Specification
7 colors, matte film

The choice of available printing and production finishes for flexible packaging is restricted by the malleable character of the material. Striking unity and a natural authenticity have been achieved in the graphic imagery across this range of potato chips as a result of the printing finish applied to a specific material. The subtle backgrounds provide a foundation on which the product title and distinctive high-definition photographic representation have been printed. The overall feel of the package is determined by the choice of finish: a matte film on which a 7-color process has been reverse-printed to produce a conspicuously natural matte finish.

DARLING SPUDS

West Country Cheddar, Leek and Pink Peppercorns

HAND COOKED POTATO CHIPS

Lovingly made, naturally flavoured

DARLING SPUDS

Fire Roasted Jalapeno Peppers

HAND COOKED POTATO CHIPS

Lovingly made, naturally flavoured

The choice of materials here is critical. Transparent plastic has a radically different finish to cartonboard, which could have been used instead, but the printing effects on a transparent surface and the ability to view the primary package inside help create a distinctive brand appearance.

RLC | PACKAGING GROUP

Project
OsiS carton

Client
Henkel KGaA

Specification
Transparent PET, black ink

These folded cartons serve as the secondary packaging to the pots within. Rather than concealing the primary packaging, these cartons have been designed using transparent PET (polyethylene terephthalate). The slick surface of the plastic complements the nature of the product, while the imagery and textual information relating to the product is printed in black ink on each side of the carton. The photographic imagery appears as a continuous band around three sides of the carton, providing an unmistakable brand identity.

WATERFORM DESIGN INC.

Project
Pill Towel point-of-sale dispenser and pill packet

Design
Designer Masayo Nai

Client
Gallery 91

Specification
2-color screenprinting, cartonboard, vacuum-formed plastic, aluminum-foil backing

Adopting the established appearance of a certain type of packaging from a completely different product sector can be a useful and sometimes cost-effective way of grabbing attention at the point of sale. Here, the blister pack, so often associated with products from the pharmaceutical industry, has been used as a device for packaging a unique gift item. The printing finish on the outer box is simple and discreet, providing a foundation on which the eye-catching production finish of blow-molded plastic sealed with metal foil on the products within is evident and clearly displayed. Each product contains four items per sheet, which are stacked within the outer box. The structural design of the cartonboard container allows the sealed box to become a point-of-sale device when opened, with the distinctive product title and logo that forms a conspicuous backdrop printed in a single color.

LET IT RUN!

Down time on the dock

1949 – Erg Training – George McCauley, Jack Russell, Jack Taylor, Bo Westlake, Herbie Simpson

PAUL HOGARTH + FLAVOUR

Project
Booklet in ziplock bag

Design
Art Director/Designers **Paul Hogarth, Briony Wilson**

Client
Argonaut Rowing Club, Canada

Specification
Waterproof Ziploc bag, screenprinting

In celebration of the 130th anniversary of a renowned rowing club, a small portable logbook was created that members could take with them whenever they rowed, giving them the option to log up to 200 results. The diminutive 64-page booklet was printed in a single color on tinted paper stock with a black cover on which the title was foil stamped above a motif of a rower. The aim of the book was to be both useful and inspirational for current and future club members. The question of how to package this reusable product was therefore a challenging one. Like the booklet itself, the design solution lay in simplicity. In deference to the sport, a waterproof opaque Ziploc bag was used, on the front of which was printed a brief and witty remark in the same typeface used on the cover the booklet. The choice of package, material, and finish, and the overall relationship it has with the product, make this an excellent packaging solution for a very specific brief.

IF THIS BAG IS FOUND FLOATING IN ANY BODY OF WATER, IT IS BECAUSE THE OWNER NEVER READ THE CONTENTS AND THUS MAY BE PRESUMED DROWNED.

PARKER WILLIAMS

Project
Sainsbury's flavored crisps

Client
Sainsbury's

Specification
Gloss, combined gloss and matte, and matte finishes

Printing finishes have been used tactically across the flagship premium-brand range of one of Britain's largest supermarket chains to aid consumer navigation and product segmentation. The reputation and stature of the brand meant that a successful solution was imperative, and this was accomplished through the use of inks and coatings, from gloss, to a combination of matte and gloss, through to matte. The design and range of printing finishes give the brand exceptional flexibility, providing a wide range of possible styles across extensive product categories.

WACKY PLASTIC

The container is manufactured using injection stretch-blow molding and wrapped in a heat-shrunk sleeve that contains all the printed information. The modified pump mechanism is injection molded and specially designed to foam the concentrated liquid during dispensing.

WEBB SCARLETT deVLAM

Project
Dishwashing foam dispensers

Client
Procter & Gamble

Specification
Injection stretch blow molding, heat-shrunk sleeve

The demanding ergonomic considerations in this innovative new pump-action soap dispenser have allowed a unique and radical aesthetic finish, yet one that is not entirely out of character in its product category in the different European and American markets. The curvaceous form has been discreetly sculpted to provide a gently contoured surface that is both visually pleasing and functionally efficient. It allows the user to dispense the product either one-handed using the ergonomic collar, or by simply depressing the top of the pump. The plastic form befits the packaging material, which offers a fresh and hygienic appearance and smooth, uncontaminated surface through which the product is displayed behind the brand identity.

WEBB SCARLETT deVLAM

Project
Filippo Berio pack

Client
Matthews Foods

Specification
Embossing, wraparound sleeve, gold ink

This distinctive package was designed for a totally new product entering a highly competitive market. The brand's premium credentials and the delivery of value in this top-of-the-range product were critical considerations in the choice of finish. The design was therefore a departure from potential competitors in this already over-crowded market, and the package's finish became a primary tool in distinguishing the product from its rivals. The overall appearance was determined by the demand among users for a "table-friendly" tub that does not look unattractively economical. The solution was a two-part package comprising a uniquely shaped container with detailed embossing and an elegant wraparound cartonboard sleeve that contains all the product information, and which can be removed and thrown away to leave only the distinguished-looking tub. The product's eminence is successfully reinforced by a number of design details, including: the addition of gold edging to the cartonboard sleeve that frames the mellow olive-green against the cream surface of the tub; the liberal use of restrained motifs embossed into the surface of the tub to emulate the work and quality of the traditional artisan and evoke Mediterranean earthenware; and the heavier weight of the material—9 oz. (25g) rather than the usual 6 oz. (17g)—a detail that provides a tactile, ceramic feel and gives the impression of quality. Users have responded positively to its deliberately clean and uncluttered finish, which reflects the core brand values of quality, taste, and authenticity.

Among the most successful decisions concerning choice of finish was not to decorate the tub and instead leave its surface refreshingly clear of printed graphics. User feedback has lauded this as evincing solidity and quality.

Eye Mask
for restful sleep when travelling
Free ear plugs included

Superdrug ☆ TRAVEL ACCESSORIES

Luggage Strap
for extra security and easy identification
on busy luggage carousels

Superdrug ☆ TRAVEL ACCESSORIES

Kwik Fix
for "on the road" repairs
The essential travel sewing kit

Superdrug ☆ TRAVEL ACCESSORIES

DAVIES LESLIE-SMITH

Project
Travel accessories packaging

Design
Art Director/Designer **Steve Davies**

Client
Superdrug

Specification
5 colors, white card, plastic clamshell, vacuum-formed blister pack

Two materials have been used in the packaging of this range of travel accessories to create a smart and functional design. The plastic blister pack is a single piece, vacuum formed and folded in half to create a void in which the product is securely contained. A card insert is positioned at the front of the void to conceal the product and display graphic information, including the product's title and a photographic representation of it. The uncomplicated design is consistent across the entire range, utilizing plenty of white space within which the product is displayed, and imagery evoking the theme of travel is arranged in a manner suggestive of the rectangular openings of an airplane's windows. The whole composition is printed using a 5-color process, with matte silver used to enhance the visual appearance of certain details.

JKR DESIGN TEAM

Project
Bassetts Allsorts packets

Client
Bassetts

Specification
Matte varnish, metallic film

The confectionary market is one of the most competitive and among the most aggressive for establishing brand presence. Being able to stand out from the crowd relies on more than just highly vivacious graphics or innovative production finishes, as constantly shifting parameters caused by new materials and printing innovations make it difficult to stay ahead of competitors for long. This eminent brand has, for decades, been among the market leaders in a number of countries by continually revitalizing its product imagery and updating the nature of its packaging, a process that continues here with this redesign of its range of bags of candies. Unlike most products in this sector of the market, which use printed plastic film as the base material for the bag, a metallic film with a matte finish has been used to provide a distinctive appearance and tactile sensation that successfully distinguishes the pack from its competitors. The natural gloss finish of the base material was used to create the gloss effect of the Bassetts Allsorts logo, with the metallic substrate showing through to achieve the golden Bertie Bassett character.

The lustrous character of the material has been cleverly exploited through the effervescent and lively design of the printed graphics. Bold white lettering on a red curvaceous background prominently displays the brand title, with the product name printed in a lively font below.

ENLIGHTENING LABELS

Displaying the necessary product information or branding on a package can often require bespoke processes that significantly increase the cost of production. The most common, effective, and efficient way of delivering customized information to standard packaging containers is the label. Labels provide a platform that can deliver product information, instructions, and branded graphics and iconography to the user without having to apply print to the surface of the primary package. In recent years the range and extent of labels has radically increased with improved manufacturing and printing processes paving the way for such innovations as the heat-shrunk sleeve, which encases an entire container in a thin film of plastic which can be printed in any number of colors and with different designs—a far cry from the time-honored adhesive paper label.

TYPICAL ANALYSIS

Calcium (Ca)	35 mg/l
Magnesium (Mg)	10 mg/l
Potassium (K)	3 mg/l
Sodium (Na)	7 mg/l
Bicarbonate	143 mg/l
Chloride (Cl)	9 mg/l
Sulphate (SO₄)	5 mg/l
Nitrate (NO₃)	5 mg/l
Dry residue at 180°C	157 mg/l
pH (at source)	7.9

L11A

Bottled at source:
Hanch England.
WS13 8HQ.
Tel: 01543 493613

Store in a cool
dry place away
from direct sunlight.
Best before:
See top of bottle.

500ml℮
www.ikea.co.uk/food

5 060085 070041 >

IKEA®
SPARKLING WATER
LOW SODIUM

WEBTECH

Project
IKEA Sparkling Water label

Client
IKEA

Specification
Transparent OPP label

Improvements in manufacturing and materials processes in recent years have had a dramatic impact on the labels industry. The market dominance of the traditional reel-fed process, by which adhesive labels are applied to a package from a reel, has been significantly reduced by the growing impact of oriented polypropylene (OPP) labeling. OPP labeling can use the same machinery as reel-fed labels, delivering the label continuously and directly from a roll of polypropylene, or can use the "cut-and-stack" method. The material has many benefits, including moisture resistance and toughness. This allows for thinner gauges of label, which in turn saves resources, and much higher speeds of application. However, the primary benefit in relation to printing is the exceptional quality of graphics that can be applied to OPP labels. This example exploits the material properties of polypropylene by using a transparent backdrop to enhance the visual impact of the printed graphics and augment the wholesome message delivered by the product. The stack of pebbles, their details and shading beautifully illustrated through the high-resolution printing, evinces the purity of the product, which is further emphasized by the clear background created by the product itself.

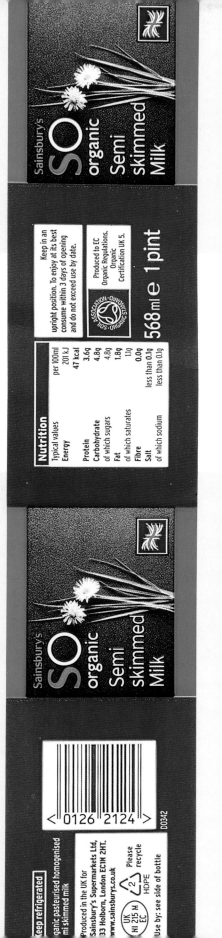

WEBTECH

Project
Sainsbury's Organic Milk label

Client
Sainsbury's

Specification
White OPP label

Oriented polypropylene (OPP) labeling comes in various forms, principally white, transparent, metallic, and frosted. The nature of the finish invariably defines the type of printed graphics that are applied to the label. A transparent label will likely exploit the color of the liquid that forms the backdrop to the printed graphics, whereas the distinctive jazziness of a metallic label will use the printed graphics to enhance the character of the material. In this example, the white background provides a clean canvas on which bold colors, a detailed photographic image, and text can be printed cleanly and clearly, giving the label a definite and fresh appearance. The choice of labeling allows for these high-quality characteristics to be achieved without any loss in image quality, which would probably have occurred if using other forms of labels, or if printed directly onto the container.

WEBTECH

Project
Sprite Zero label

Client
Coca-Cola

Specification
White OPP label

A major advantage of oriented polypropylene (OPP) labeling in the context of the production process is the speed at which labels can be applied to the container and the thin gauge of material, which significantly reduces the quantity of material used. This gives designers a little more freedom to work with larger areas for little added cost to production. Large labels are often employed in the carbonated drinks market, especially for larger bottles, to arrest customers' attention in a highly competitive market where bright colored products and dazzling graphic imagery is the norm. This example uses white polypropylene as the base for a conspicuously effervescent design whose printed finish delivers a sharply detailed image. This degree of clarity and detail delivered in large quantities at high speed is obtainable only by using OPP labeling.

A key benefit of OPP labels is their moisture resistance, so when the product is spilt by an overzealous consumer, the integrity of the label and the printed graphics are not compromised.

WEST ISLAND GROUP

Project
Biddenden Cider bottle

Client
Biddenden Vineyard & Ciders

Specification
Polypropylene label, matte-UV varnish

Choosing a finish and appropriate design for labels is rarely simply a question of aesthetics. This polypropylene label is used on a bottle containing cider. The label had therefore to withstand the extreme temperatures subjected to it during pasteurization and to remain on the bottle throughout the process of bottling. A very strong adhesive that fixed polypropylene to glass without compromising the visual and physical qualities of the label was sourced. A nonabsorbent wipeable matte-UV varnish was chosen to seal the label's outer surface.

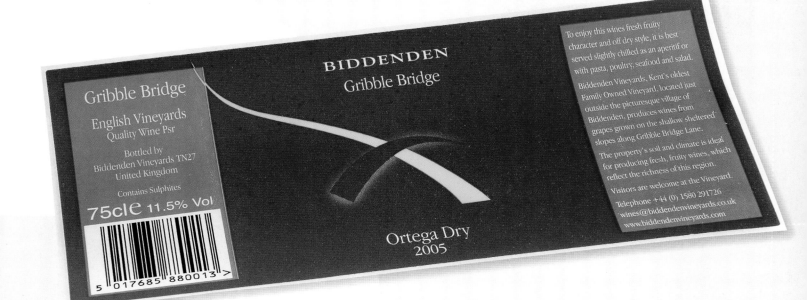

DRAGON ROUGE

Project
Perrier bottle

Design
Art Director/Designer **Patrick Veyssière**

Client
Perrier

Specification
Offset lithography, aluminum paper, vitrophany

Rare instances of brilliance in structural or graphic design can produce packaging that becomes a classic in its own right and that helps to forge the identity of the brand. Whether through the shape of the package, the design of the graphics, or the unique color scheme, design classics provide infrequent glimpses of genius in an industry often criticized for its mediocrity. The physical character of this glass bottle, whose graceful, voluptuous curves reflect the purity and form of a drop of water, the very product it contains, has helped to define the brand's identity—an identity that is recognized around the world. The bottle's memorable green is replicated in the label, whose graphic design has been subtly updated, yet remains indisputably part of a brand genealogy spanning decades. Aluminum paper provides the base for the printed graphics on the neck of the bottle, augmented by a subtle detail on the back, where a historical monogram has been printed in vitrophany (giving a mirror image) on an elliptical adhesive label intended to be viewed from the front of the bottle. The overall composition of the physical and graphic design displays an unmistakable minimalism and distinction that has survived generations and will no doubt continue for many years to come.

VITRO

Project
Coca-Cola Blak bottle

Client
Coca-Cola

Specification
Heat shrunk plastic sleeve

A minor revolution in packaging finishes for bottles occurred with the introduction of new manufacturing processes that allowed containers to be entirely enshrouded in plastic sleeves. The sleeves, which are applied over the bottle and heat-shrunk for a permanent fit, offer the graphic designer an extraordinary degree of creative freedom to determine the visual appearance of the bottle. Improved technologies and techniques have reduced the extent to which the design, particularly the typography, is distorted by the heat-shrinking process so that now almost no distortion is caused when the label shrinks to the contours of the bottle.

DRAGON ROUGE

Project
Eau de Perrier label and bottle

Design
Art Director/Designer **Patrick Veyssière**

Client
Perrier

Specification
Stretched cold sleeve label, PET bottle

With a well-established and distinguished bottle leading this product range, there are ample opportunities for the brand to diversify into different product variations and packaging solutions without undermining the strong core character of the brand. This variation draws on the same central themes that have made the brand famous: the curvaceous bottle (here slightly elongated), the minimalist appearance, clean graphics, and overriding visual simplicity. Evident deviations from the original product are the material, its blue hue, and the modern imagery. Graphics have been applied to the PET (polyethylene terephthalate) bottle through a stretched plastic sleeve that envelops it. The overall cleanness of design and elegant form are intended to make this an attractive and desirable accompaniment to the dinner table.

VITRO

Project
Diet Coke bottle

Client
Coca-Cola

Specification
Heat-transfer label, contoured bottle

A production finish can, in rare cases, make such an impact and be so successful as to define the brand identity. Few glass bottles are as instantly recognizable around the world as the Coke bottle. So distinctive is the curvilinear form that it has become widely acknowledged as a design classic. The root of this design lies in the molding: the designer has incorporated both a curvaceous profile and subtle detailing suggestive of segments around the bottle, so giving it a tactile quality that adds to the bottle's already excellent ergonomic characteristics. The means of displaying product information has changed considerably over the decades. Formerly, the brand's title was embossed on the bottle, but with the introduction of new technologies, the finish has altered markedly, with paper, plastic, and heat-transferred labels all being used. In this instance, the label is a heat-transfer applied to an even band around the center of the bottle. The bottle is sealed with a metal crown cap.

DESIGN BRIDGE

Project
Fernando de Castilla sherry bottles

Design
Creative Director **Graham Shearsby**
Designer **Antonia Hayward**

Client
Fernando de Castilla

Specification
**Embossing, 4-color process plus 3 specials, gold foil,
textured self-adhesive paper**

Labeling is often the designer's best, and
sometimes only, opportunity to present the
appropriate character for a product packaged
in glass bottles, as the high costs incurred by
bespoke production mean that many products
are packaged in generic bottles. This heightens
the role of good label design and, budget
permitting, choice of closure in delivering the
distinctive branding or product characteristics.
The design of the labels in this range has
captured the eminent character of this high-
quality brand by using a distinctive tactile
paper with deep-embossed details. The nature
of the paper evokes the distinguished quality
of handmade papers, with their mottled and
uneven surfaces. This refined character is
reinforced by the elaborate embossed fonts
that dominate the center of the label. The soft
shade with which they have been printed has
the subtle distinction of a watermark, though
the drop shadow provides a visual clue that
the motif stands proud of the label's surface.
The product title at the base of the label has
been printed in black at the smallest readable
font size so as not to undermine the overall
delicate appearance.

DEPENDABLE PAPER

Ever since our ancient ancestors first realized
that packaging helped preserve and protect food,
organic fiber-based materials have been the
most common and trusted for the purpose.
Today, fiber-based board exists in a perplexing
array of different weights, structures, finishes,
and laminations. From the humble corrugated
board used for transit packaging to the lavishly
coated cartonboards used for luxury-goods
packaging; from the complexity of the multi-
layered drinks carton to the carefully crafted
handmade gift wrapper, paper offers a packaging
solution that is immensely diverse and eminently
dependable. The physical properties of fiberboard
make it a challenging and rewarding material
to design with, and since the raw material of all
paper-based packaging is wood, the material
is both sustainable and recyclable.

FLIPFLOP DESIGN LTD.

Project
Con Moto box and bottles

Design
Art Director/Designer **Lee Saxelby**

Client
Marks & Spencer

Specification
1-color offset printing, ridged carton, matte and gloss UV varnishes

Achieving a visually arresting design does not necessarily demand the use of a riot of color, a cocktail of varnishes, or gaudy graphics. This range of cosmetics uses only the offset printing of black ink on white cartonboard to create the design, with a combination of matte and gloss UV varnishes to enhance its effect. The simple yet highly effective finishes are founded on the French Renaissance–inspired print, which is designed to appeal to both male and female markets. Black patterning on a white background has been reversed on the side of the carton in a clever variation that gives strength to the carton and helps to visually lift the lighter-toned lid. The distinctive pattern appeals to modern tastes by reflecting contemporary trends in interior design. This theme is maintained in the matte and gloss varnishes that have been applied to echo textures within the home. The combination of black and white as the basis for the visual identity of the brand is continued with the containers concealed within the outer carton, which are wrapped affectionately in white paper and tied with black ribbons with white-dotted trim.

Superdrug
Pewter Hip Flask
Funnel included
Stain resistant

Superdrug
Mini Torch
High intensity light beam
Anodised aluminium

Superdrug
Compact Pedometer
Calculates steps, calories and distance

DAVIES LESLIE-SMITH

Project
Outdoor accessories gift boxes

Design
Art Director/Designer **Tim Leslie-Smith**

Client
Superdrug

Specification
5 colors, white cartonboard, satin varnish

White cartonboard provides a clean, uncluttered foundation for displaying the printed graphics on this range of outdoor products. Printed in a 5-color process, the products are partially displayed on the front face of the container in a manner that illustrates their most notable characteristics and their surface finishes in close detail. The High Definition Printing is augmented with a metallic blue spot color to produce distinctively striking highlights, and coated with a satin varnish to give the container a smooth finish that is silken to the touch. While the printing of this package uses a full palette of colors, it also demonstrates the importance of white space and how effective it can be to avoid the temptation of overusing the full-color process.

MAYR-MELNHOF PACKAGING AUSTRIA

Project
Côte d'Or Oraïa Christmas box

Client
KRAFT foods

Specification
Structural relief embossing, gold ink, gold lamination, hot foil stamping, tapered square cut, crash lock, 4-color process plus 2 Pantone inks, varnish

The same techniques used in the package opposite are retained in this package, offering a consistency that underlines the brand's identity. However, this package has a more festive feel than its rather austere sibling. This has been achieved through the prominent gold patterning on the lid and upper sides, which, by being suggestive of fireworks, evoke celebration. This is emphasized by the vertical design of the package, which contrasts with the horizontal design of its counterpart.

MAYR-MELNHOF PACKAGING AUSTRIA

Project
Côte d'Or Oraïa box

Client
KRAFT foods

Specification
Structural relief embossing, chamfering, lens-shaped lid, hollow-frame base, 4-color process plus 2 Pantone inks (outer surface), 1 color, food-safe ink (inner surface), hot foil stamping, varnish

Light embossing to the top half of the front of this box creates a distinctive physical effect. This, combined with the tanned dappled print, gives an impression of quality, evocative of leather. These reassuring tones are continued on the interior of the box. The application of spattered gold highlighting on the lower half of the front provides a very different textural experience that complements the top half and offers an appealing foundation on which the product can be strikingly displayed in the center of the package. Attention is also drawn to the product through the well-considered use of the red logo banner that points to the product name, embossed in gold, and the image of the product itself. Beneath the red banner a series of bands in red and gold feature the product name and emulate ribbons that run around the package, navigating their way around the corners and chamfered edges.

WHITESPACE

Project
Hotscotch Sauce bottle, tube, and leaflet

Design
Creative Director **Iain Valentine**
Designer **Claire Morrow**
Artworker **Ricky Bentley**
Photographer **Niall Hendrie**

Client
The Scotch Malt Whisky Society

Specification
4-color process, GF Smith Accent Antique and 150gsm
Colorplan bright white paper stock, powder-coating

The finishes employed on this package and accompanying leaflet were inspired by the product's ingredients and reflect the refined qualities of its manufacturing process. A key component of this process requires the use of oakwood casks to achieve the product's distinguished character. The unifying facet of the different elements of the design is the distinctively speckled wooden grain of oak that provides a natural and uniquely textural quality to both the outer container and the label of the bottle. Scorched into this grain is the product title, which appears on both elements of the packaging. The product title and its woodlike appearance were faithfully reproduced from an original photograph, requiring high-definition and full-color printing to maintain the necessary level of detail. To further augment the grainy surface, a textured stock was selected for the outer container. The cohesive character of the primary packaging has been achieved intelligently, with the product's rich colors corresponding with the tones of the label and the black screw-cap lid mirroring the burned qualities displayed in the product title.

Striking red tones have been used on the metal lid and base of the outer container to reflect the fiery qualities of chilli, one of the product's key ingredients. The same scheme has been used on the reverse of an accompanying leaflet, which is covered entirely in chilies printed in a full-color process so that when the outer container is opened, the bottle appears to be enveloped in chilies.

MAYR-MELNHOF PACKAGING/ JUNKER DESIGN AGENTUR GMBH

Project
Lacalut toothpaste tube

Client
Etol Gesundheitspflege und Pharmaprodukte GmbH

Specification
Metallic silver ink, gloss finish, embossing, hot foil stamping

The product's key attribute is evoked through the distinctive use of silver metallic ink in a bright gloss finish suggestive of freshness, cleanliness, and brilliance. The choice of font and colors maintains this connotation through the use of deep blue, vivid red, and white highlights. The nonmetallic finishes and the use of embossing around the brand's name further complement the appearance and help lift the graphic information from the vivacious background.

FUELHAUS

Project
Michael's Cookies gift box

Design
Creative Director **Ty Webb**
Designer **Etel Garaguay**

Client
Michael's Cookies

Specification
Arjowiggins Curious Metallics paper stock, metallic ink, 4-color process, spot colors, embossing

A complete visual makeover transformed what was originally a white cartonboard container into this distinctive package, which boasts a range of printing and production finishes employed to reflect the premium character of the product. The printing effects include spot metallic and PMS (Pantone Matching System) inks applied to silver paper stock. The parallel lines of color contrast strongly with the silver base and are reflected in the detailing on the container's lid, which is printed 4-color process. Spot UV varnishes in a speckled pattern on the silver surfaces provide an element of visual detailing intended to echo the character of the product's uneven surface.

Embossing of the brand logo helps it to subtly rise from the silver surface of the container—enough to be noticeable, but not so much as to undermine the uncluttered visual composition of the overall design.

MAYR-MELNHOF PACKAGING INTERNATIONAL

Project
Sainsbury's tissue box

Client
Kimberly-Clark

Specification
Holographic printing, fluorescent pink ink, textured stock

Some product types adopt lurid colors and typography to attract attention. Laundry detergents, a prime example, have been doing this for decades. This package, however, is from a market sector that more commonly employs soft pastel tones to reflect the gentle nature of the product. The design and finish confidently buck this trend by using a printing finish that grabs attention through a striking combination of holographic printing and fluorescent pink ink. The effect is boosted by the variegated surface, which reflects the light in a dramatic manner.

Product information and a symbolic reference to the softness of the product are displayed on a matte-pink banner on the front edge of the package, which contrasts with the glossy and highly effervescent setting.

DAVIES LESLIE-SMITH

Project
Seafood & Eat It containers

Design
Creative Director **Tim Leslie-Smith**

Client
Seafood & Eat It

Specification
4-color process, white cartonboard, satin varnish

This series of cartonboard containers for a selection of seafood products uses simple materials and printing techniques to produce a classic, clean, and tempting appearance across the product range. Printed with a 4-color process on white cartonboard, the distinctive visual appearance is created by the contrast between the crab device in front of a backdrop of radiating lines and the solid block of black on which, in bold white, is displayed the product title and supplementary information. A satin varnish provides the carton with a smooth finish, in keeping with the fresh character of the printed graphics. The distinction between products in the range is achieved simply through the application of different colors in the upper part of the package and the separate product title below.

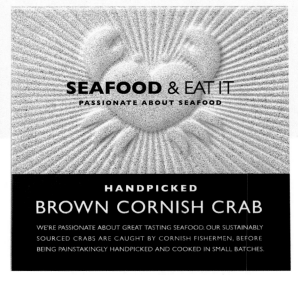

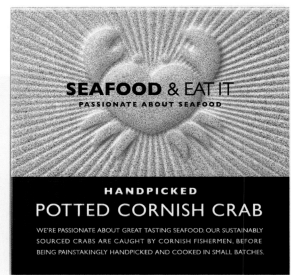

MAYR-MELNHOF PACKAGING INTERNATIONAL

Project
Traumhafter Advent calendar

Client
Stollwerck

Specification
Perforation, folding, flat-pack, tray insert

The copious perforations and folds in this flat-packed Advent calendar allow the packaging, through a simple transformation, to become the product. The careful synchronization of production and printing insures that when assembled the three-dimensional package appears like a stage set, in this instance depicting an Arabian scene. The color scheme throughout the whole product is warm and welcoming. This is continued on the inserted tray that houses the confectionary beneath each window, so that when all the windows are opened the effect is not diminished. The deep-blue sky, in contrast, provides an intense backdrop to the scene.

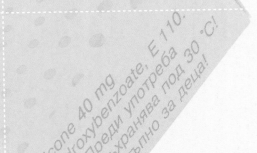

25 Kapseln · Zum Einnehmen

Espumisan®

Simethicon · Bei Blähungen

BERLIN-CHEMIE
MENARINI

1 Kapsel enthält Simethicon 40 mg
Enthält Methyl-4-hydroxybenzoat, E 110.
Packungsbeilage beachten!
Apothekenpflichtig · Nicht über 30 °C lagern!
Arzneimittel unzugänglich für Kinder aufbewahren!

1 капсула съдържа Simethicone 40 mg
Съдържа още methyl parahydroxybenzoate, E 110.
Без лекарско предписание! · Преди употреба
прочетете листовката! · Да се съхранява под 30 °C!
Да се съхранява на място, недостъпно за деца!

RLC | PACKAGING GROUP

Project
Espumisan box

Client
Berlin-Chemie AG

Specification
Cold-foil enhancement, high-gloss coating on 275gsm
GC2 Tambrite

The foil detailing on this cartonboard container is applied using a technique called cold-foil enhancement. This technique means the foil can be applied inline, so offering much greater accuracy of registration as well as allowing it to be overprinted with up to six UV inks and two coatings. All this improves the creative potential of foil in graphic design, thus giving designers the opportunity to make use of effects that were not previously possible.

RLC | PACKAGING GROUP

Project
Cerrus aftershave carton

Client
Maxim Markenprodukte GmbH & Co. KG

Specification
Iriodin pigments, embossing, high embossing

The striking quality of this package, created by the solid blue tones and textured finish, helps enhance brand identity and offers the user a unique visual and tactile experience. The deep-blue color, which is created by Iriodin pigments, evokes the "ocean" in the brand's name. The scheme goes further still by using specialized embossing to create a wavelike effect on the surface of the carton, giving the package an unmistakable and memorable tactility. The application of a soft white shadow behind the brand name helps lift this important graphic component from the surface of the package and further supports the notion that the text is floating above the surface of the sea. As a whole, the choice and application of finishes convey the feeling, scent, and effect of the product while successfully communicating the sense of revitalizing freshness that the brand is all about.

DEPENDABLE PAPER

WHITESPACE

Project
Totseat boxes

Design
Creative Director **Iain Valentine**
Artworker **Ricky Bentley**

Client
Totseat

Specification
1 color, 350gsm single-sided packing board, die-cutting

This cartonboard container replaced a plastic pouch package that was deemed less effective in delivering the shelf presence the product demanded. Therefore, the new design was conceived to have a strong presence. The rigid structural qualities of cartonboard allow the product to be bulk-stacked in retail outlets, presenting the product information clearly, and also acting as a promotional device. Each face of the cube possesses a distinct finish and displays a different piece of information, presented either as a photograph of the product in use; in bold typography; or physically, by die-cutting circular windows in the board. This range of visual messages is particularly effective when the containers are displayed en masse; the whole composition comprising an array of patterns, forms, and colors. Since the product is sold internationally, careful consideration was given to the artwork and how it might be perceived in different cultural and linguistic contexts. The solution was to print the standard artwork on all packaging and overlay this with adhesive labels in different languages for the various markets in which the product is sold.

The die-cut window serves not only as a visual device to help distinguish the different faces of the cube, it also allows customers to view the fabric of the product without having to open the container.

RLC | PACKAGING GROUP

Project
Curad bandages box

Client
Beiersdorf AG

Specification
Silver hot-foil embossing, 6 colors, inline UV varnish, 225gsm GC2 Tambrite

A distinctive and high-quality finish has been employed in the design of this packaging for an upscale brand of adhesive bandages. Silver—a key characteristic of the product and the primary marketing attribute of the brand—is evinced through the extensive and elegant use of silver and silver-green colors on the front of the package. This exceptional finish is achieved by using 6-color process printing, hot-foil embossing, and inline UV varnishing. The graphic representation of the product is tastefully illustrated, highlighting the silver ingredient with a glinting highlight in the front corner of the product. The strict hygiene standards demanded by this product are insured by a security seal on the package that requires a perforated device to be broken before the product can be accessed, and an ingenious closure system maintains product protection after the seal has been broken.

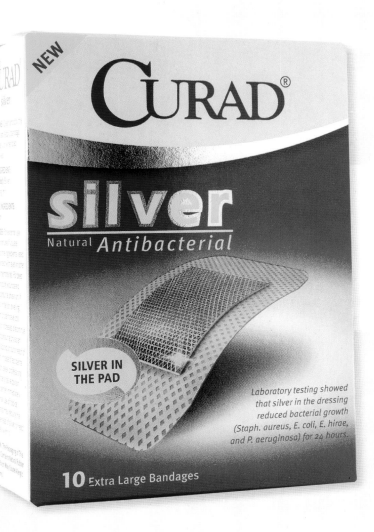

DEPENDABLE PAPER

CHESAPEAKE CORPORATION

Project
Sainsbury's pudding carton

Client
Matthew Walker for Sainsbury

Specification
Fiber cartonboard, 265gsm Iggesund Incada Exel, sheet-fed offset lithography, 6 colors, 2 inline varnishes, flat-bed cut-and-crease, embossing

The range of finishes available to packaging designers working with cartonboard is already diverse and getting ever broader as new techniques are perfected. This trial package was created to illustrate the use of twin-varnish effects. The results were considered to be successful enough for the technique to be used on a range of commercially available products. The carton has an overall "soft-touch" matte finish, giving it a tactility that complements and contrasts with the high-gloss spot detailing that lifts the tag designs from the surface of the carton and suggests they are separate components from the main package.

The highlights and varnish effects on the ribbons that "wrap" around the box and are tied in bows on the front give this feature an exceptional authenticity. All the effects and printing were applied in a single print pass on a 6-color offset-litho press.

The identity and flexible finish has been designed to work across multiple products, including bars, boxes, tubs, jars, and limited-edition products.

PEARLFISHER

Project
Green & Black's chocolate wrappers

Client
Green & Black's

Specification
Spot varnish, bespoke brown ink

The influence of a printing finish should never be underestimated. In the most exceptional circumstances it can play a central role in the phenomenal success of a brand. Such was the experience of this well-known chocolate. The new packaging took the sumptuously rich tones of the chocolate bean and created a unique shade of brown exclusive to this brand. While this shade formed the foundation for the brand, as the range increased, each new flavor was defined by a new colored band. The defining finish is created by layers of typography and subtle uses of spot varnishing that communicate quality and luxury. Organic becomes a supporting message to taste and premium appeal, and, since the redesign, sales have increased sevenfold.

DEPENDABLE PAPER

WEST ISLAND GROUP

Project
Van Gils Eau de Toilette carton

Client
Fine Fragrances

Specification
Spot-UV varnish, debossing, embossing, silver foil blocking

Spot-UV varnishing and embossing—or, conversely, debossing—are two simple techniques commonly used, sometimes concurrently, by designers and printers to visually and physically "lift" the details of a design from the surface of a package. The effect of a varnished highlight draws attention to the varnished area as well as providing a markedly different tactile quality, while the physical appearance of embossing and debossing can add a sense of finesse to an otherwise bare surface. In this example, both debossing and embossing have been used, combined with a spot-UV varnish, to add a greater emphasis on the horizontal bars that wrap around the four sides of this carton. To emphasize further the graphic details of this design against the deliberately unadorned background, silver foiling has been applied to the lettering.

The graphic design has necessitated a very tight register of spot-UV varnish between the narrow bars, requiring a great deal of precision at the printing stage.

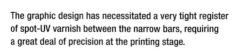

WEST ISLAND GROUP

Project
Montezuma's chocolate box

Client
Montezuma's

Specification
Laminated cartonboard

Materials technologies have greatly enhanced the designer's palette when considering the range of finishes available. Where in the past it might have been necessary to consider using two or even three independent materials to achieve the required physical and functional requirements of a package, composites, such as laminated paperboard, allow designers to use just one. Traditionally, packaging for chocolate bars used foil wrapping to insure that the product maintained its freshness, while an outer paper wrapper contained the branding and product information. This range of packaging for a new make of chocolate has carefully considered the choice of material to preserve the integrity of the product, to assist in differentiating the product from competitors, and to provide a unique finish that leaves a lasting impression on customers.

A laminated cartonboard has been designed to provide a printable surface on one side and a foil layer on the other that provides the necessary barrier protection.

ELECTRIC DESIGN

Project
Geoplan software packaging

Design
Senior Designer **Matthew Shaw**
Consultant Designer **James Day**

Client
Geoplan Spatial Intelligence Ltd.

Specification
1 color, 170gsm matte board, matte lamination,
folding boxboard, die-cutting, hand assembly,
3M double-sided tape

Strikingly clean printing and various subtle production techniques have been used throughout this range of software products to create a pristine finish in line with the product's reputation. The product range comprises four individual CDs plus a user guide for each. A number of factors had to be taken into consideration when undertaking the structural design for the separate packs, including maintaining a strong sense of brand identity across the range, using the same basic components to prevent prohibitively high manufacturing and printing setup costs, and accommodating the different thicknesses of the user manuals. The brand identity has been assertively and skillfully imposed through the use of a range of printing and production techniques. The printing is consistent across the range, using a single distinguishing tone—the same tone as that used in the product's corporate identity—printed onto 170gsm matte art paper that has been matte laminated to give a silky and "wipe-clean" finish. Physical treatments have also been used to reinforce a coherent identity, including the consistent use of rounded motifs, which are most conspicuous on the front face of the outer sleeve. This attractive series of patterns serves various purposes that go well beyond providing just an aesthetically pleasing finish; they also offer a means of telling each product apart while augmenting the sense of brand identity. Each package contains at least five components: outer sleeve, inner box, frame, plinth, and insert. The outer sleeve is untainted by overt printing and displays only the physical attributes of the die-cut pattern and the product titling discreetly positioned in the top-left corner. When the outer sleeve is removed, the inner box is revealed, which contains a printed insert concealing and protecting the manual beneath. This sits on top of the CD, which is snugly encased in a folded frame and sits on a folded plinth. A small tab protrudes from the plinth to allow the CD to be removed easily without damaging the package. The inner box, plinth, frame, and insert are all made from 1/32in (700 micron) folding boxboard. In all but the premium product, which has a thicker user manual, an additional piece of 5/16in (8mm) twin-flute corrugated cardboard sits beneath the plinth to compensate for the space created by the thinner user manuals, and prevent the contents from rattling around inside the package.

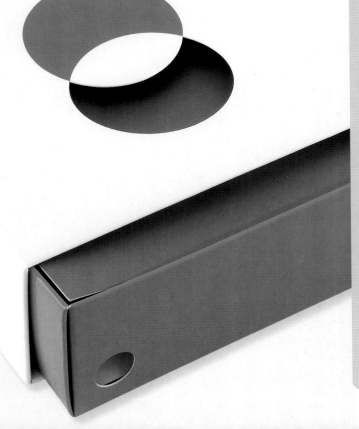

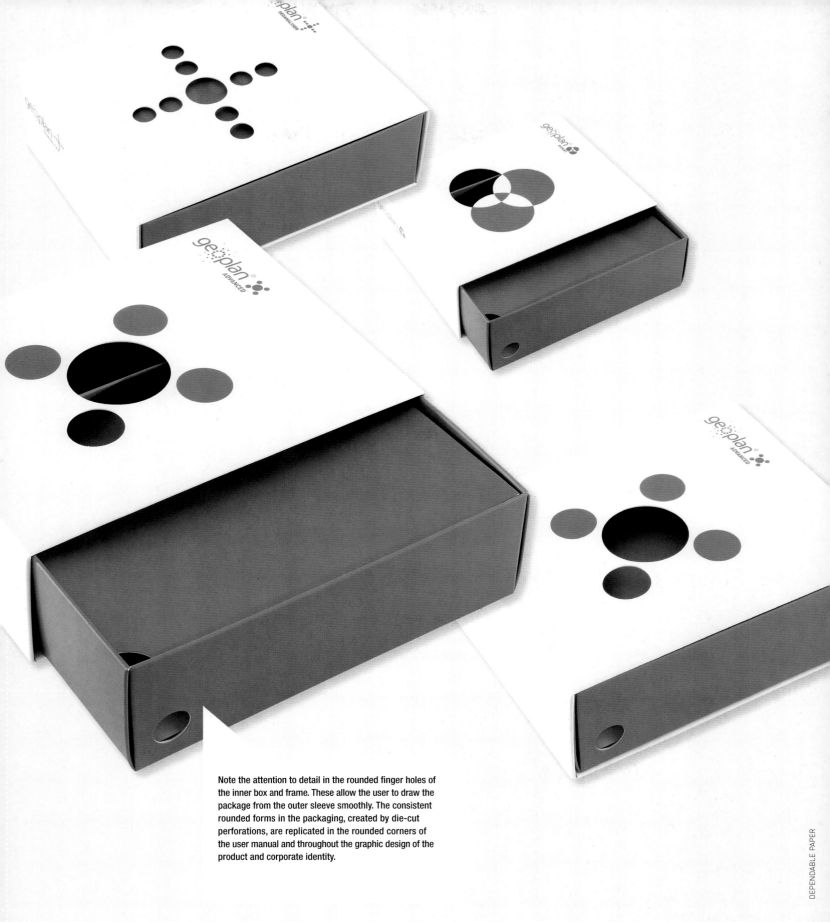

Note the attention to detail in the rounded finger holes of the inner box and frame. These allow the user to draw the package from the outer sleeve smoothly. The consistent rounded forms in the packaging, created by die-cut perforations, are replicated in the rounded corners of the user manual and throughout the graphic design of the product and corporate identity.

JKR DESIGN TEAM

Project
Gillette & The Art of Shaving box

Client
The Art of Shaving

Specification
Matte lamination, foil blocking, spot-gloss varnish, opaque ink, metallized board, lithography

This gift package comprises a number of separate components that contain and present the range of items inside in a highly attractive, visually striking composition. Each component has been given a distinctive printing treatment to create an appealing and distinguished appearance both when the package is open and when it is closed. The outer sleeve performs the primary means of presentation, while the inner trays contain and protect the products within. Printed in a plain base coat finished with a matte lamination, the outer sleeve appears clean and refined, and the only decorative elements are the logo and product titling. Spot gloss varnishing and foil blocking have been applied to these details to elevate them from the solid color of the background and present a strong visual message to the consumer. The metallic theme is stronger on the inner trays, which withdraw from both ends of the sleeve. A small cutaway section at the base of the outer sleeve reveals a small portion of these inner trays, the thin stripes of which can be seen gleaming below the product name. The high-gloss metallized board with printed matte stripes used in both trays creates a dynamic visual effect and contrasts strongly with the matte-laminated outer sleeve to create a prominent ensemble that evokes the precision and hygienic characteristics of the product and its function. An inner board with lift-out brochure printed in the same color as the outer sleeve sits in one of the trays.

GREEN HOUSE DESIGN CO. LTD.

Project
Hanaguruma flower wheels

Design
Designer/Illustrator **Kaori Murakami**

Client
Oribe Co. Ltd.

Specification
3-color offset printing, matte varnish (Patent Registered Hanaguruma Package Shape Design)

Different cultural contexts provide rich pickings for designers seeking innovative solutions, and this paper container was inspired by the Japanese art of origami. Through a series of regular creases, a flat, circular sheet of paper can be folded to create a rounded container of varying depth that can be used in a wide range of packaging contexts. The production finish, which uses recurrent folds that meet at the top of the container in an attractive floral arrangement, is very striking. When the container is open, the spiraling folds present an attractive display that neatly exhibits the product contained within. A functional aspect of the packaging is that, when open, it serves as a plate from which the product can be consumed, making it an ideal package for food. The printing in this example has been kept minimal, portraying soft gradients and floral patterns in pastel tones produced by 3-color offset printing with a matte varnish. To enhance the imagery, the printing was applied to the reverse side of the coated paper in order to achieve the appearance of the traditional Japanese paper known as washi, which is made from plant fibers that give it a distinctive translucent appearance and tactility. Though this container is relatively simple to produce, its visual and structural appearance is complex, providing an exceptional opportunity for graphic designers to produce striking printed finishes that evolve as the container is opened and the folds reveal the full extent of the design.

JKR DESIGN TEAM

Project
Molton Brown Color Cosmetics boxes

Client
Molton Brown

Specification
Matte lamination, gloss-UV varnish, bronze cartonboard

Printing finishes have been used across this collection of distinguished cosmetics products to give the product range a collective unity and reinforce the strong sense of brand identity. The distinctive neutral tone of bronze printed on coated cartonboard provides a natural and wholesome quality to each package, but also provides a foundation on which the classic serif typeface of the brand is printed in a slightly darker tone. Though the intricate font is subdued by the subtle difference in shading between it and the background color, it is lifted from its setting by the application of spot varnishing. This shiny characteristic contrasts with the matte texture of its surroundings, emitting an almost subliminal brand message and providing a dignified appearance. The product title and logo are displayed neatly in a pallid tone in the corner of the primary face of each pack.

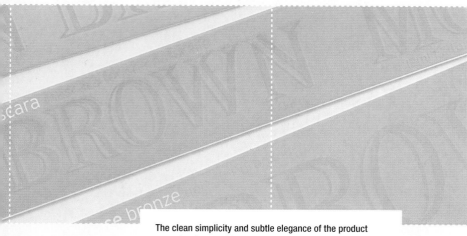

The clean simplicity and subtle elegance of the product range has been achieved by the careful choice of materials and printing finishes. The inner packaging in each container preserves this delicate composition by using plain white cartonboard that does not detract in any way from the outer packaging. Less, in the design of this range, is definitely more.

GREEN HOUSE DESIGN CO. LTD.

Project
Akebono lunch box

Design
Designer/Illustrator **Kaori Murakami**

Client
Oribe Co. Ltd.

Specification
4-color process, gloss varnish

The printing technique on this fast-food package is designed to imitate the traditional Japanese technique of lacquering known as akebono, which literally means "dawn." Where a black lacquer is usually applied as a base overpainted in red, which can be removed to reveal the black, this represents the reverse process, where red lacquer is used as a base and black is painted on top. As the black is removed, the red emerges from underneath to evoke the dawn. A 4-color printing process has been used to create, in realistic tones, the patterning of this traditional technique, with a gloss varnish applied as a finish to imitate the high-gloss lacquered effect of Japanese craft products. The base of the cartonboard container is printed in a reversal of the lid, with a red overlay on a black foundation. Inside, the box is divided up by a gold-painted folded cartonboard insert.

GREEN HOUSE DESIGN CO. LTD.

Project
Sikinohana celebration box

Design
Designer/Illustrator **Kaori Murakami**

Client
Oribe Co. Ltd.

Specification
4-color process plus white opaque ink, OP varnish

This strikingly beautiful box, designed for a celebratory gift of food, was inspired by traditional Japanese painting and screen-printing. At celebrations in Japan it is customary for people to receive a small gift, and a dish of red rice—made by steaming rice with red beans, which gives it a distinctive reddish tint that is symbolic of celebration—is a traditional offering. The distinguished nature of the product demands an attractive appearance, and this has been achieved by recreating detailed and elegant traditional design using an innovative treatment of modern printing techniques. The flower designs are produced in a 4-color process on top of white opaque ink to give them their vibrant appearance against the gold base, which was produced not by using gold-coated cartonboard but by printing yellow ink onto silver-coated board. The whole design was OP (oxidative polymerization) varnished to provide a good seal to the surface, which also offers excellent resistance to scratching and friction, perhaps through excessive movement during transportation. Inside, a transparent plastic dish contains the food to protect it from the outer packaging and to prevent the outer packaging being soiled by the food.

GREEN HOUSE DESIGN CO. LTD.

Project
Miniature cake tray

Design
Designer/Illustrator **Kaori Murakami**

Client
Oribe Co. Ltd.

Specification
OP varnish, 2-color and 1-color offset lithography

A tidy composition has been created for this gift parcel for cakes by combining a simple structural design of cartonboard with the printing of discreet graphic designs. The two-part container consists of a tray and an outer sleeve, keeping the printing costs low while making a highly attractive package whether open or closed. The outer sleeve in both designs have been offset printed in three colors with an OP (oxidative polymerization) varnish, while, inside, the trays have been printed in just one and two colors. These can be removed from the sleeve and used as standalone presentation trays, making the structural and graphic design of the tray an important element of the overall package despite being concealed at the point of sale.

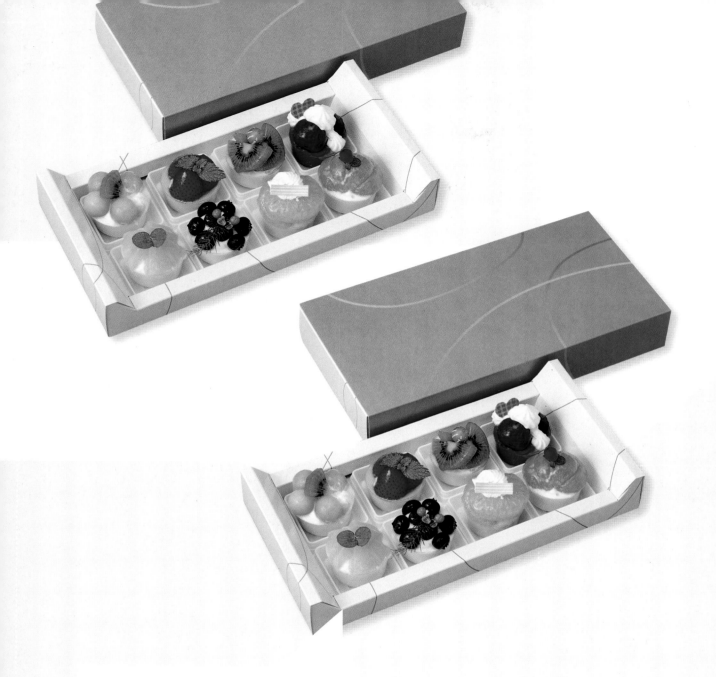

The ends of the trays have been structurally designed so that the package is sealed when closed, thus maintaining the products' freshness, but it is also a device by which to grip the tray if passing it around among guests.

GREEN HOUSE
DESIGN CO. LTD.

Project
Bottle gourd lunch box

Design
Designer/Illustrator **Kaori Murakami**

Client
Oribe Co. Ltd.

Specification
4-color process, gloss varnish

Traditional Japanese blockprinting was the inspiration for this design for a take-out lunch box. The time-honored lacquering technique of maki-e is renowned for its speckled appearance; it is created by applying gold powder to a base layer of wet lacquer to create a luxurious finish. Four-color printing and an overlay of gloss varnish on a base of black ink here attempts to reproduce this powderlike texture. The specially commissioned blockprint design of Japanese bottle gourds and leaves overlaid on a grid pattern, which evokes a trellis, creates a distinctive and beautiful exterior. The base of the container is also printed with leaf patterns and continues the latticework effect to provide continuity to the composition when sealed. Inside, a series of partitions to separate the contents are created by gold-printed folded cartonboard.

HELVETICA

Project
Kanebo can

Client
Kracie Home Product

Specification
Metal paper, matte- and gloss-UV varnish

A majestic appearance has been achieved in this design through the highly sensitive application of materials and varnishes that subtly but sensuously evoke a distinction and beauty befitting the product. The color and the floral design are repeated on both the product and the outer packaging, producing an eminent and distinctive whole. On the cartonboard container the lines of the floral design are brought out by a spot varnish, while the voids are left matte. This combination produces an outstanding effect in which the lines of the flowers shimmer with reflections against a backdrop of deep red. The white text, in Japanese and Chinese characters as well as Latin script, sits discreetly along the edges of the container's front face, adding a certain artistic character to the overall composition. Inside, the product uses the same technique of contrasting gloss varnish and matte, but in reverse—the lines of the pattern are printed matte against the gloss voids in a band around the middle of the container. The base of the container has been left bare while the upper portion is reserved for the lid. To distinguish the lid from the base, a slender gold trim has been applied to the lip.

The choice of materials augments the printed finish by using brushed metal, which provides a matte, tactile finish. The band of gloss patterning across the center of the container offers the user a contrasting tactile experience.

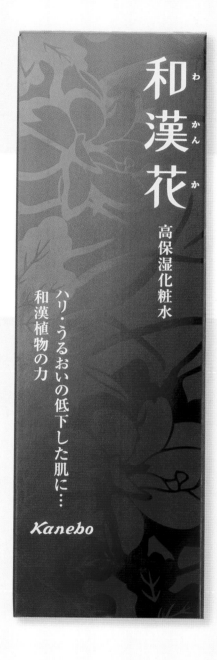

HELVETICA

Project
Pasticcino Dolce box and tubs

Client
Hotel Nikko Tokyo

Specification
Matte paper, matte varnish, gloss hot stamp

Designed for a renowned boutique hotel in Tokyo, this series of packages aims to evince the exclusive interior and luxurious atmosphere of the hotel. The product is comprised of four elements: the outer cartonboard container and three cylindrical drums that contain confectionary. Visual detailing has been kept to a minimum on the outer container, with only the product name and title appearing centrally among a series of vertical stripes of pale yellow and white. The finish is deliberately understated in order to allow the viewer to savor the more elaborately decorated packaging within. The three drums of confectionary sit side-by-side in the rectangular outer container. Duotone photographic imagery provides the predominant visual theme, setting the tone of the products and the sense of distinction of the establishment they represent. Each drum is made from dense fiberboard and contains a lid that can be removed by pulling on a fabric tag in the center of the top of the lid. The lids have been left white except for the printed text and logo, which duplicate the information on the front of the outer container.

A matte finish has been applied to the bases and lids of the cylindrical drums to convey a sense of simplicity and quality. The choice of matte and gloss finishes is an important one that designers must often make, as either can represent higher- or lower-end finishes depending on how they are applied and on which materials they are being used. In this case, the dense fiberboard, the quality of the photographic imagery, and the manner in which the lids smoothly slide from the bases of the cylinders suit a matte finish, so evoking a sense of quality and understated charm.

The presentation of the product has been carefully considered in the structural design of the cartonboard container, so that when opening it the products are revealed in a dignified and formal manner.

HELVETICA

Project
Hefti Jeunesse chocolate box

Client
Böögg Japan

Specification
Gloss paper, vacuum-formed plastic tray, transparent film

A combination of materials and finishes has been used to create an upscale appearance for a Swiss product aimed at a Japanese market. The two different sizes of package use the same design principle of a printed outer cartonboard container and an inner vacuum-molded plastic tray to securely house the products, which are kept fresh within a transparent, sealed plastic wrapping. A number of different production finishes are used in the three different materials that make up the package, but it is the printing finish that is primarily responsible for evoking the product's character and prominence. The range of sensuous brown tones in a striking pattern of different-sized crescents overlaid upon a base of deep chocolate-brown is highly suggestive of the product's alluring and appetizing characteristics. A large dark-brown circle with an inner circle of lighter brown provides a platform on which the product title and supplementary information can be displayed clearly but discreetly in white. A matte finish has been applied to the outer container to retain the textual quality of the cartonboard and to reflect the silky character of the product.

HELVETICA

Project
Hefti Jeunesse ice cream tubs

Client
Böögg Japan

Specification
Polypropylene film on gloss paper

This range of frozen products from a Swiss chocolatier designed for sale in Japan has had to consider how the distinctive attributes of the product should be portrayed to a receptive market, but one in which the ingredients and flavors used might be unfamiliar. The coated cartonboard container has been given a printing treatment that is eminently attractive in its own right, but equally and classically geared to Japanese taste through the use of pale colors and measured graphic patterns. Soft tones printed in a single color—different for each flavor—on a white background produce a finish that distinguishes each product type while retaining a unity across the entire range. Foremost in establishing this sense of brand cohesion is the application on each design of a band of printed gold with a textured silky finish, suggestive of brushed metal, around the rim of the lid, which affirms the brand's distinction and underlines a sense of excellence. The color on the tub's base is repeated on the top of the lid to complete the consistent and venerable presentation of the overall package.

QUALVIS/BIGFISH DESIGNERS

Project
Rack of lamb box

Client
Waitrose/Dalehead Foods

Specification
Gloss varnish, high-quality photography

The strength of a message often depends on the way a package communicates visually with the user. Here, the nature of the product is both a potential strength and weakness—while cooked meat can evince a sense of quality and eminence, it has an appearance and tactility that attracts admirers and detractors in equal measure. The chosen finish of this package draws attention to the product's superior characteristics by photographing it in subdued lighting against a plain, dark, background and, most importantly, it is a very high-quality reproduction. The photograph's narrow depth of field further helps concentrate attention by giving the front of the product exceptional detail and clarity that blurs rapidly as it moves toward the background. The subtle use of a reflection provides further visual cues, especially a sense of cleanliness, which is reinforced by the gloss varnish that coats the entire package. The necessary text has been kept to a minimum so as not to clutter the overall crisp, clean composition.

The high quality of the photography and its reproduction on the package creates a distinguished appearance that is preserved and enhanced by the minimal use of additional graphics as well as the clean finish that the gloss varnish provides.

The chosen finishes help support the key product attributes and principal selling point—the hand-decorated icing—through the use of photography, a gloss varnish finish to lift the decorative motifs, the distinctive appearance of decorative and script typefaces, and, most importantly, the die-cut window that permits views of the product.

QUALVIS

Project
Christmas cake boxes

Client
Tesco/Beaverlac Fine Foods

Specification
High-quality photography, die-cutting, gloss finish

A number of different techniques have been employed here to present a clear visual and emotional festive message. The celebratory character is established by a patterned base that is bedecked with merry Christmas motifs and finished in a mixture of dark tones and contrasting subdued golds. Set against this comforting backdrop are clearly defined boxes containing the product information, which are deliberately lighter in color and contain either text or photographic reproductions of the product. The choice of font in the text boxes is deliberately elaborate in order to present a sense of superior quality. While the photos of the product perform a useful and visually appealing function, consumers are also given a view of the product through the large die-cut window on the upper side of the box, which is the principal feature of the package. The uniform outline of the window is broken only by the two boxes—one containing product information and the other a signature stamp—that encroach into the top and bottom edges of the die-cut window and subtly draw the eye to this information without detracting from the product. The gloss finish helps provide a glint to the overall package that befits the occasion.

QUALVIS/BIGFISH DESIGNERS

Project
Gü and Frü boxes

Client
Gü Chocolate Puds

Specification
Light varnish, High Definition Printing

The products' distinctive and appealing qualities are the basis for the finishes in this range of premium deserts. From the sumptuous earthy tones of chocolate in one design to the invigorating clarity of the icing that tops the product in the other, the finishes clearly reflect the products' key attributes. High Definition Printing faithfully reproduces a photographic image of the product, which has been positioned centrally on each face of the four-sided carton. Graphic content has been kept to an absolute minimum, with the brand's bespoke sans-serif font clearly declaring the product's name while retaining the overall pure and uncluttered appearance. The light varnish gives the outer surface of the packages a soft, visual, and tactile sheen. The structural design, characterized by the wide square base tapering to a rounded closure, also adds to the product's unique appeal and helps distinguish it from competitors.

QUALVIS

Project
The Square Pie box

Client
Bigham's Pies

Specification
1 color plus black

Sophistication and complexity in printing and production finishes are not always desirable objectives, as a simple appearance can provide a raw appeal suggestive of frankness and honesty. This design deliberately plays on this leaner approach, keeping the packaging material exposed and using its warm tones and textural quality to augment the character of the product. The graphics complement this style unambiguously by using minimal printing, in this case, one color plus black, to produce bold blocks of color that display the product's title as well as echoing the physical character of the package. Black ink has been used sparingly in the product description to complete the economical and reliable image created for this heartily utilitarian product.

295g ℮
steak &
mushroom
all natural classic pie
DISPLAY UNTIL
USE BY
KEEP REFRIGERATED,
SUITABLE FOR FREEZING
square pie
steak & mushroom
love your pie

ENVIRONMENTAL ESSENTIALS

Few issues are more critical than the sustained safeguarding of the environment. Technological advances in materials, printing, and manufacturing processes are constantly delivering improvements to lessen the impact that packaging has on the environment and to enhance the way it performs throughout its entire lifecycle. These include the lightweighting of materials through improved design and materials, the development of new organic composite materials to replace resource-dependent alternatives, and improved structural and systems design in the delivery and recovery of products and packaging materials during and after their useful life. The designer is central to delivering these environmental improvements, presenting the profession with constant but, ultimately, profoundly rewarding challenges.

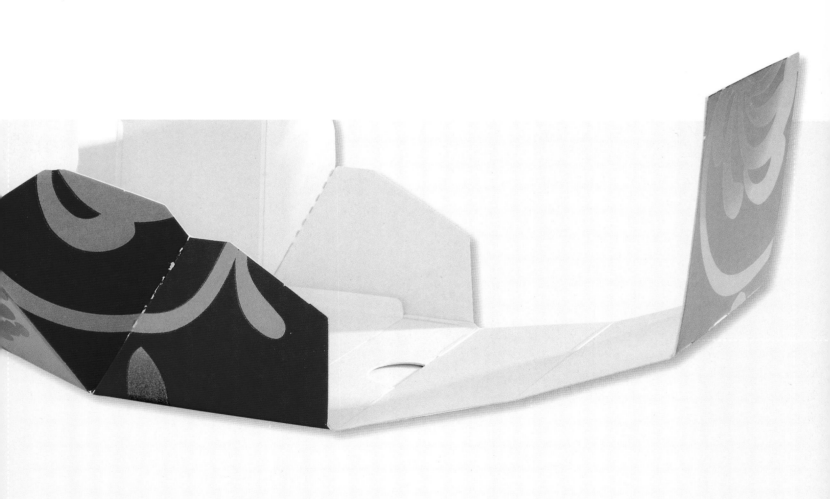

CHESAPEAKE CORPORATION

Project
Sainsbury's pudding sleeves

Client
Matthew Walker for Sainsbury

Specification
**Primary fiber cartonboard, 285gsm Iggesund Incada
Exel, sheet-fed offset lithography, Metallix system**

Environmental issues have long been a major concern in packaging, but few sectors of the industry have responded with genuine and lasting commitments. In recent years there has even been a recidivist trend toward overpackaging by some, a lapse that few would have considered possible a decade ago. One of the lesser-known problems that can have an adverse effect on the environment is the use of inks, millions of gallons of which are manufactured and consumed by the packaging industry every year. In an attempt to reduce pollutants caused by ingredients in metallic paint, the Metallix system (patent pending) has been developed to offer strong metallic effects without the need for metallic inks or metallized substrates. This package has been printed using this new technique, giving a distinctive sparkling effect behind a solid band of color on which the product information is displayed.

Additional graphic detailing has been applied in raised patterns that give the package an inviting tactile quality. These details float above the highly visual sparkling base coat to present a distinctive celebratory character.

Sainsbury's
Taste the difference

Rum Nicky sponge pudding
A traditional sponge pudding with a **hint of ginger**, topped with plump rum soaked raisins and **crunchy demerara sugar**, to give a delicious alternative pudding.

Best before end

CHESAPEAKE CORPORATION

Project
Sainsbury's pudding sleeves

Client
Self-initiated

Specification
Sheet-fed offset lithography, 285gsm Iggesund Incada Exel, Metallix system

This sample design demonstrates the remarkably vibrant metallic effect achieved by the Metallix system (patent pending), which contains no metallic inks or metallized substrates. The subtle use of highlighting, shading, and careful choice of colors further enhances the dazzling effect produced by this new technique. The environmental benefits go beyond eliminating potentially polluting metals in inks, as it can be applied to standard fiberboard, which means that it can be used in place of the metallized polyester-laminated cartonboard that is commonly used when applying metallic effects to that substrate.

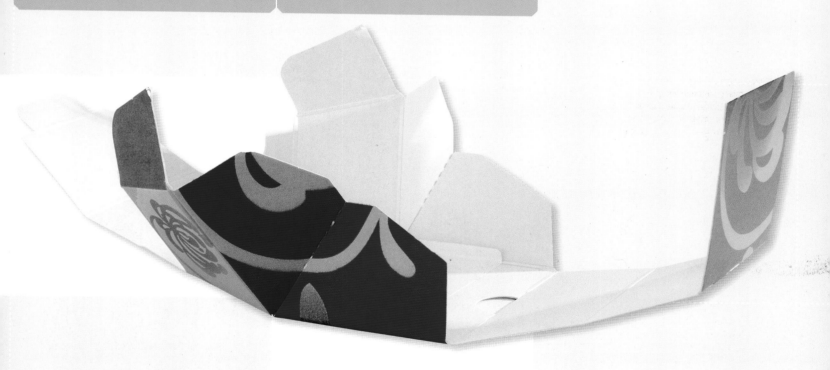

HUHTAMAKI

Project
Recycled polyethylene terephthalate (RPET) containers

Client
Self-initiated

Specification
RPET, clip lid, relief-plate printing, spot color, UV paste inks

Because plastics depend on a nonrenewable source for their manufacture, they have a poor ecological image. In response, the plastics-packaging industry has aimed to clean up its act by reducing the content of plastic packaging through improvements in design, materials technologies, and manufacturing processes. However, one area that is still in its infancy and yet has huge potential is the recycling of postconsumer-waste plastic materials. If plastics can successfully be collected and reused, rather than dumped or incinerated to create energy, the lifecycle of the material is greatly extended, and the impact on the environment potentially reduced. This has not been done in the past because systems of collection have not been efficient and the properties of postconsumer materials have been poor. But this is changing. Recycled polyethylene terephthalate, or RPET, has been manufactured by Huhtamaki, one of the first companies in the world to introduce thermoformed food packaging made from this new material. RPET is derived from recycled PET bottles, the standard material for soft-drinks containers. These thermoformed salad packs contain between 40 and 70 percent postconsumer PET, yet maintain the same performance characteristics—such as excellent clarity, good crack resistance, and outstanding gas-barrier properties—as virgin material. These containers are film-sealed to maintain product freshness and a level of tamper evidence, and they come with a clip lid onto which printed graphics can easily be applied.

The shape of each package has been carefully considered to insure maximum efficiency during transportation and shelf storage, further improving environmental benefits.

HUHTAMAKI

Project
PLA cup

Client
NatureWorks LLC

Specification
**PLA plastic, relief-plate printing, spot color,
UV paste inks**

Plastic has been used as a packaging material for decades, but, despite its environmental benefits, it remains vulnerable to claims that its dependency on nonrenewable resources makes it unsustainable. Challenging this claim had been difficult until the introduction of biodegradable plastics, the technologies for which have improved drastically in recent years. Now there is a material on the market which boasts such exceptional characteristics that users can barely distinguish between the biodegradable and nonbiodegradable packages. Produced by NatureWorks LLC, the new material, PLA (polylactic acid), is 100 percent biodegradable yet possesses outstanding clarity and thermoforming properties, thus meeting the most rigorous demands for textured surface finishes and printing. At last designers no longer have to compromise their environmental credentials to deliver a wide range of finishes in plastic.

SOMETHING SPECIAL

The packaging of items for special occasions
invariably entails a little extra consideration
on the part of the designer and a slightly more
generous budget on the part of the client. This
usually presents designers with far more creative
freedom than other packaging briefs and offers
exciting opportunities to experiment with a wider
range of materials and printing processes. The
very nature of gift packaging demands a little
extra flare from designers to not only raise the
profile of the package above the competition on
a commercial level but also, on a personal level,
to serve as a suitably desirable product in its own
right for the recipient.

RICE DESIGN

Project
Macallan Valentine's Day bottle

Design
Art Director **Shizuko Ushijima (Suntory Co. Ltd.)**

Client
Suntory Co. Ltd.

Specification
Paper box, 4-color process, art-coated paper

Gift packaging, with shorter production runs and larger budgets, often gives designers the opportunity to be more adventurous with their designs and the materials they use. This gift box for a miniature bottle of a renowned brand of Scottish liquor was aimed at discerning Japanese consumers. The box intended for this culturally specific market was constructed in cartonboard. Using a lithographic process, the high-quality finish reproduces the subtle shades and gradients of finely polished marble, thus giving the container a distinguished appearance and upholding the eminence of the brand. A fabric tab on the side of the hinged lid clearly indicates how the container opens. On the underside of the lid the contents of the box and history of the product are printed in two languages. Inside, the structural design of the cartonboard safely holds the product and a souvenir glass, so that, once the lid is opened, views of the label and branding are clearly visible.

PRINT AND PRODUCTION FINISHES FOR PACKAGING

RICE DESIGN

Project
Jack Daniel's Valentine's Day bottle

Design
Art Director Shizuko Ushijima (Suntory Co. Ltd.)

Client
Suntory Co. Ltd.

Specification
Paper box, satin cloth, transparent plastic lid, 4-color process, art-coated paper

Uncomplicated printing and manufacturing processes have been employed to create a visually complex composition suggestive of a quality and refinement befitting this famous brand of American whiskey. A range of different materials and printing finishes are used in this gift box. The strong brand identity has been left visible from beneath the transparent plastic cover, which has been left clear except for the renowned title and description printed in a single color in the center of the cover. A slender outline, also in the same gold print, frames the printed graphics and products beneath. The base of the container is solid black, mirroring the well-known brand identity on the label of the bottle. The materials within the container have been carefully chosen to evince a sense of quality, with the bed of black satin providing a sumptuous platform on which the presentation bottle and gift glass lie.

Without the cost of additional printing or manufacturing processes, the luxurious finish of this gift box is strongly influenced by the choice of materials, particularly the base of satin. The brand identity is reinforced not only through the use of the black fabric but also in the subtle swirling highlights and shadows that cleverly evoke the curling lines of the patterned frame on the black-and-white label.

RICE DESIGN

Project
Valentine's Day chocolate box

Design
Art Director **Eijiro Kuniyoshi**
(Kotobukiseihan Printing Co., Ltd.)

Client
Kanou Sho-jyuan Co. Ltd.

Specification
Wooden box, Japanese paper, string, transparent seal, matte gold print

There are few packaging applications more deserving of a little extra care and attention than the design of a box of chocolates for Valentine's Day. This design employs a number of different materials and finishes to produce a restrained and eminently superior package appropriate to the special occasion. The box is housed beneath a thin sheet of wood, the organic texture and natural patterning of which presents an individual and notable statement. In the center the brand logo has been applied using a transparent adhesive label. The same logo appears in the center of a similarly square and pale but much smaller card containing the product information. The soft, natural tones are repeated throughout the printing of the box and the outer wrapping of handmade paper with inlaid petals and pressed flowers. A cord of brown string binds the whole container, finishing the package in a dignified and personal manner.

FLIPFLOP DESIGN LTD.

Project
Perfection bottles and box

Design
Art Director/Designer **Lee Saxelby**

Client
Marks & Spencer

Specification
Ridged gold foil, vacuum-formed insert, foil blocking

The packaging of two premium products in a single container provides the opportunity to produce a conspicuously glamorous gift box that not only fulfills the functional requirement of safely containing and protecting the individual products, but also presents them in a stylish and striking manner that adds value and a sense of distinction to the brand. The two-part outer container is comprised of a base manufactured from ridged gold foil, and a transparent plastic lid with gold print in the center displaying the product name. The gold theme is continued thoughtfully on the solid black vacuum-formed insert with the printing of swirling patterns in thin lines of gold ink. The rich contrast of black and gold and the shimmering reflection that occurs on the internal sides of the gold foil carton present an air of sophistication and glamor that helps to set this product apart from potential competition in the marketplace.

Note how the structural design has produced a manufacturing finish that enhances the product's quality by doubling the thickness of the outer walls and the inner partitioning walls of the container. Not only does this improve the appearance of the overall design, it also provides an additional functional role by making the package stronger.

RICE DESIGN

Project
King of Himalaya Tea box and sachets

Design
Art Director **Takuya Hara**
(Kotobukiseihan Printing Co., Ltd.)

Client
Tsuboichiseicha Co. Ltd.

Specification
Paper box, tant (matte) paper, gold bag, 2 colors

The finishes used for this exclusive packaging containing three sachets of premium tea were chosen because they deliberately and explicitly evoke the regal character of the brand and the distinction of the product. A single-color process has been used to print the solid wash of mid-gray on the outer cartonboard container, providing a neutral and solid foundation that enhances the shimmering gold-foil sachets by contrasting starkly in tone, texture, and hue. The gold of the sachets presents a dazzling and superior finish that suits the nature of the product and the message it imparts.
To complete the composition, a band of paper with the product description and branding, printed in the same base of solid gray as the outer container, is used to wrap around each sachet, augmenting the product's elegance. These bands have been printed in a 2-color process, with yellow ink being used for the text and providing a neat, patterned trim to the edges of the band that harmonize with the golden finish of the sachets.

RICE DESIGN

Project
Commemorative sake box and bottle

Design
Art Director **Hiroko Yamakawa**
(Kotobukiseihan Printing Co., Ltd.)

Client
Choryo Brewing Co. Ltd.

Specification
Paper box, paper label, gold seal, gold Japanese paper, neck-rolling paper, special foil paper, seal deposition paper, label art paper, 2 colors

Bottles of spirits are often packaged in presentation cases to heighten their sense of quality and exclusivity. Such cases are usually made of metal or cartonboard, both materials that provide distinctive qualities and benefits in the range of printing and production finishes they can achieve. Here, a coated corrugated board has been used. The printed finish on the outer container mirrors the graphics on the label of the bottle and the dark color of the glass, making both containers unambiguously related. Despite these well-balanced characteristics, the distinguishing feature of this design is the use of a silver-foil cover over the cap of the bottle, closed with a patterned string. This added detail and choice of materials provides a hallmark and helps elevate the distinction of this brand above its competitors, increasing its presence and reinforcing its identity.

An adhesive gold label, reminiscent of a traditional wax seal, secures the string to the bottle, creating a distinguished appearance and a functional, tamper-proof means of insuring the product's integrity.

WEIRD AND WONDERFUL

Not all packaging employs the familiar materials of glass, plastic, paper, and metal. Some products allow peculiar packaging solutions, while others allow the use of bizarre materials. While the outlandish is often difficult to achieve when mass produced, smaller production runs or one-off designs can allow designers to consider bespoke packaging that can take the job out of the familiar and into the realm of the weird and the wonderful. These rare opportunities present designers with a chance to flex their creative muscles. This not only provides an often refreshing change from the constraints imposed on more usual packaging briefs, but may also serve as a catalyst to unlocking creative potential that can, in turn, be used in other packaging solutions.

JORGE JORGE

Project
Manuel Carvalho 30th anniversary gift package

Design
Art Director/Designer **Jorge Jorge**

Client
Manuel Carvalho

Specification
Textured velvet, paper, foil stamping

To mark the 30th anniversary of the company Manuel Carvalho, a special package containing a CD and book was created to present to guests at the celebrations. High-quality, superior effects were essential to the design, and the exterior of the box was finished in a textured fabric, presenting a highly sensuous effect that is tastefully and fittingly enhanced by foil stamping the signature motif in gold. Dominating the ornamentation is the number "30," denoting the anniversary and the purpose of the package, which is tempered by the curvilinear patterns that frame the device. Inside, both the book and the CD are cushioned in a velvet platform. The box opens along the front edge, hinging along the back edge, to reveal the contents, which are sumptuously embedded in velvet.

The gold and elaborate patterning in the centered logo is fittingly contrasted with the unadorned fabric background, creating a classic appearance that is appropriately restrained and eminently desirable.

Project
Aluminum ring

Design
Art Director/Designer **Peter Crnokrak**

Client
Self-initiated

Specification
Reclaimed clear condiment packets, clear matte adhesive sticker, adhesive aluminum tape, vegetable oil, hand assembly, offset printing

Packaging jewelry often demands a unique design solution that befits the precious character and quality of the product. The packaging for this distinctive piece draws inspiration directly from the characteristics of the product and its unusual choice of materials. Aluminum, commonly used for a wide variety of industrial and commercial purposes, is rarely used as a base material for jewelry. The decision to exploit aluminum's durable and eye-catching properties has resulted in a piece that playfully challenges perceived notions of what is precious and what is commonplace. The faces of the ring have been deliberately left unprocessed to retain the rough matte-gray finish of industrial aluminum, while the outer surfaces and ring hole have been highly polished to produce a mirror finish. The customized packaging reflects the characteristics of this material and the production techniques that have helped distinguish its surfaces by accommodating the ring in a clear plastic condiments packet submerged in what appears to be machine oil. This witty reference to the product's distinctive character and the production processes that have forged it has created a highly individual packaging solution that augments the product's own distinctive qualities. Four materials have been used in the packaging: a plastic molded packet; vegetable oil (a nontoxic alternative to machine oil) inside the packet; and a clear matte self-adhesive sticker and self-adhesive aluminum tape to seal it.

Because printed graphics could not be
applied directly to the aluminum tape,
offset printing has been used to apply
the necessary product information directly
onto the adhesive sticker that overlays
on the tape.

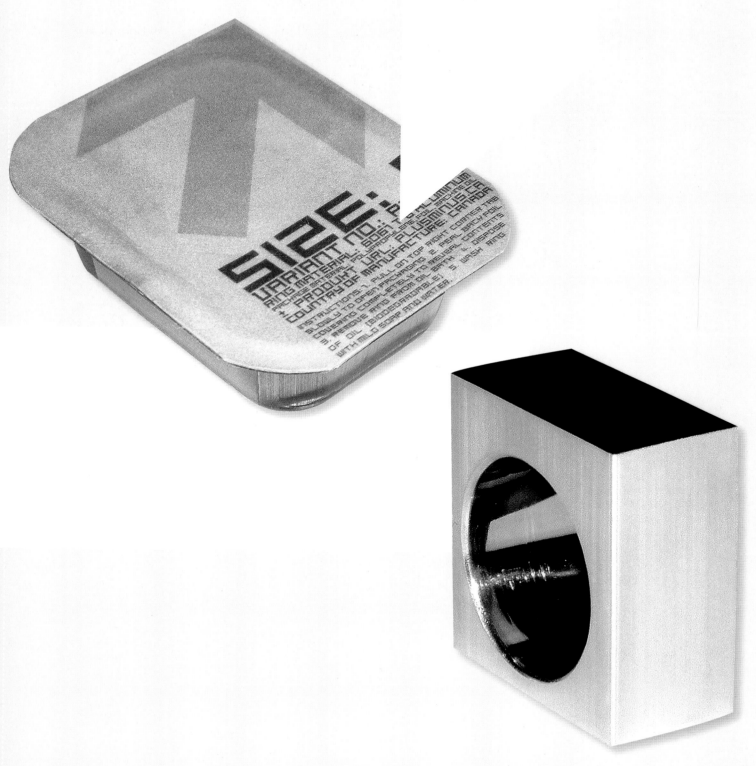

HOTSPOT MAP ×1
HOLDING PAGE ×3
INFO. + CURTAIN ×7
FAVICON ×1
XTR. PATTERN ×5
SITE PATTERN ×13
SITE BUTTON ×12
SITE BANNER ×2
SITE CALENDAR ×1
HYPERTEXT
PATTERN ×12

±

Project
Software box

Design
Art Director/Designer **Peter Crnokrak**

Client
Mobile Digital Commons Network

Specification
Recycled CD trays, offset printing, 118gsm matte Accent
Opaque Smooth, microdot perforation

Packaging for CD-ROMs, as distinct from
music CDs, rarely draws much attention
from designers beyond the application of
graphics on booklets inside the CD jewel
case or directly onto the outside of the box.
However, the design for this CD-ROM uses
an alternative packaging that deliberately
plays on the idea of the product contents.
The disk contains a graphics-standards
manual for printed and web-based applications
associated with a project that examined wireless
technology. The choice of packaging materials
was therefore influenced entirely by the product
in both a humorous and thought-provoking
device. A premanufactured electrostatic box
containing foam inserts to protect the digital
information provides the primary protection,
but a disused CD tray serves as a means of
securing and presenting the CD-ROM in a way
that emphasizes the nature of its contents.

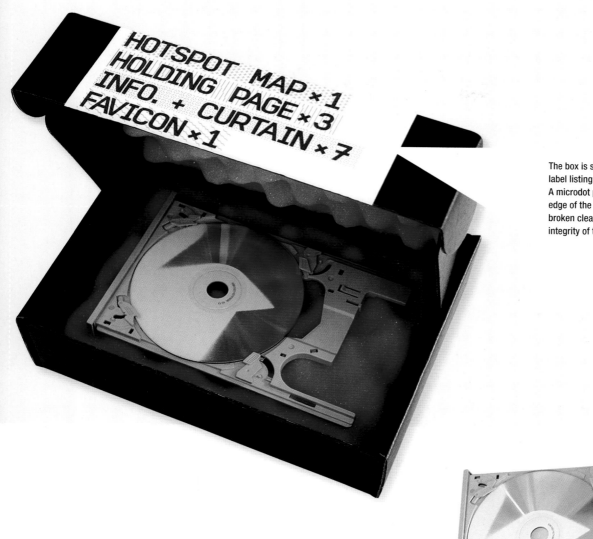

HOTSPOT MAP × 1
HOLDING PAGE × 3
INFO. + CURTAIN × 7
FAVICON × 1

The box is sealed with a plain adhesive label listing the contents of the CD-ROM. A microdot perforation along the opening edge of the box allows the label to be broken cleanly, thereby preserving the integrity of the printed information.

CONTENTS LIST /
CD TRAY + CDROM
LOGO + TYPE × 6
WORDMARK + GLYPH × 3
STATIONARY × 1
TYPEFACE × 5
PDF TEMPLATE × 3
HOTSPOT MAP × 1
HOLDING PAGE × 3
INFO. + CURTAIN × 3
FAVICON × 1

WEBB SCARLETT deVLAM

Project
SmartMarket SmartTray

Client
Self-initiated

Specification
Conceptual design

This conceptual range of packaging for the year 2020, called SmartMarket, has been designed in an attempt to confront the predicted obesity epidemic in Western society and anticipate future packaging applications. This particular example attempts to make school nutrition not only healthy and tasty but also "cool" by promoting the acceptability of healthy food within a given peer group. The system was designed for school canteens, and its aim is to educate children about the food they eat so they become interested in nutrition and their health. Each package would contain a portion of food that is distributed to the user from a central location. Radio-frequency identification (RFID) tags on each dish would provide feedback to climate-controlling technology in order to keep the food at precise temperatures and humidity levels, so guaranteeing its freshness during distribution and storage. The tags would also be capable of storing information about the nutritional value of the food, and, at the canteen, when the user selects the food they wish to eat, this information will be "read" by an electronic scanner in the SmartTray and passed to the user along with their long-term dietary record.

As technology improves, packaging will inevitably become more responsive and interactive, and this will have profound effects on the types of finishes available to packaging designers. Packaging that delivers information to the user or from which information can be downloaded, or packaging that changes its form or color according to its environment, are new parameters that designers should begin to consider.

WEBB SCARLETT deVLAM

Project
Empathy pill dispenser

Client
Self-initiated

Specification
Conceptual design

Technological developments will soon be able to deliver more than just bizarre forms and extraordinary printing techniques. Improvements in digital technologies will allow packaging to respond to the user "intelligently." This conceptual container has been conceived for the future dispensation of drugs for everyday illnesses—it would not be considered suitable for medication for serious or life-threatening ailments. Though currently not viable, the project opens designers' eyes to the potential of future packaging actually to serve and respond to the needs of the user. The design aims to guide compliance and transmit empathy toward the user as an integral part of the therapeutic process. It presupposes a number of projected factors, including pharmaceutical manufacturers supplying programmed memory chips with the drugs they sell and the evolving role of the pharmacy to become a data hub that electronically programs dedicated packs automatically while dispensing drugs. The pack comprises two parts: a reusable main body—incorporating the dispensing-gate mechanism, the display, and the majority of the electronics—and a disposable activator dedicated to a specific drug. Once activated, the pack is ready to "talk" to the patient in an appropriate manner. If a patient forgets to take a pill, an alarm reminds them; if the patient increases the dose, the pack adopts an empathetic role. For example, in the early stages of flu, the pack is calm, sympathetic, and encouraging through imagery, color, the rate at which these indicators change, and text. As health improves, the imagery becomes more positive and upbeat. Conversely, if the patient deteriorates—indicated by increased dosing—it responds appropriately. The pack also has the capability to suggest ways to encourage the curative process.

The purpose of this type of conceptual design is to free the designer's mind of perceived norms and consider the wealth of opportunities presented by existing or imminent technologies. The idea that a package's finish can actually change in response to user needs and assist the user may no longer be science fiction.

USEFUL RESOURCES

Materials

Art paper
See Coated stock.

Cartonboard
A fiber-based material of varying weights used extensively in consumer packaging for its excellent structural and printing properties.

Coated stock
A smooth, hard-surfaced paper good for reproducing halftone images. It is created by coating the surface with china clay.

Corrugated board
Highly ridged board made up of layers of flat and corrugated paper for excellent strength and rigidity. Often used for primary packaging.

Crown cork
The metal closure, usually with rubber insert on the underside, used to seal the tops of glass bottles.

Folded boxboard
See Cartonboard.

Heat-shrunk sleeves
Preprinted plastic film applied over the surface of a container and then heated to shrink over the surface, completely enveloping it and creating a permanent label.

High-density polyethylene
A high-tensile thermoplastic used extensively in the packaging industry for uses ranging from plastic bags to rigid containers.

Low-density polyethylene
Very tough thermoplastic used in a wide range of packaging applications from connector rings for multipack drinks cans to coating containers in order to provide a transparent barrier protection.

Metallized film
Laminated film composed of layers of plastic and metal. The metal film provides either decorative (shiny effect) or functional (barrier protection) properties.

Oriented polypropylene labeling (OPP)
Strong and moisture-resistant plastic labeling that can be applied at high speeds in cut-and-stack and, specially, reel-fed processes.

Polyethylene terephthalate (PET)
Thermoplastic used extensively in the bottling industry for its strength and barrier properties.

Polypropylene
A flexible plastic sheet available in many different colors, including clear and frosted.

Pressure-sensitive labeling
Labels produced with three layers: paper, transparent adhesive, and backing. When the backing is removed and pressure is applied, the labels will adhere to most surfaces.

Pulpboard
Uncoated board made from wood pulp.

Radio-frequency identification (RFID) tags
Tags that can be affixed to a product or package that contain electronic data that can be read by a receiving device. Ideal for containing product information or for use as security tags.

ROPP closure
"Roll-on pilfer-proof" closures are among the most common means of sealing bottles. The threaded closure around the neck of the bottle has a series of small perforations that fracture when the cap is unscrewed, leaving a band of material around the neck of the bottle as evidence that the bottle has been opened.

Shrink-wrap film
A clear plastic film that is heated so that it shrinks and seals around a product or container to form a tight-fitting layer.

Stock

Another word for the paper or board used to produce a design.

Uncoated stock

Paper that has a rougher surface than coated paper, so it is both bulkier and more opaque.

Vinyl labeling

Plastic adhesive material, available in many colors.

Molding

Blow molding

See Injection blow molding, Stretch blow molding, and Extrusion blow molding.

Extrusion blow molding

Similar to injection blow molding, but the material is extruded into the mold cavity and blown under lower pressure before cooling and ejection, which allows for a wider range of surface textures in the surface of the final bottle.

Injection blow molding

Manufacturing process used to mass produce plastic and glass bottles by means of injecting the material into a hollow mold and blowing compressed air through a core rod so that the material inflates to the sides of the mold to form the shape of the bottle.

Injection molding

Method of forming plastic by means of injecting molten resin into a sealed mold.

Punt

The indentation underneath the base of a glass bottle.

Stretch blow molding

Similar to injection blow molding, but the material is preformed and heated and shaped through both blowing and stretching. The stretching process increases the material's strain resistance, making SBM particularly suited to applications where the bottle must resist high pressures such as those created by carbonated liquids.

Vacuum molding

Thermoforming process in which a heated plastic sheet is formed into shapes by being stretched and held over a mold by a vacuum. Also known as vacuum forming.

Printing

Bespoke Pantone colors

Colors created by mixing inks together to form an individual color that does not appear on Pantone referencing charts. See also Pantone.

CMYK

See Full color.

Ceramic labeling

Application of ceramic inks directly onto the surface of a glass bottle through a screenprinting process.

Duotone

Where two colors are printed together to make an image richer and denser in color.

Full color

Almost all mass-produced print uses lithographic inks. As a rule, full-color printing is achieved through the combination of four process colors: cyan, magenta, yellow, and black/key (CMYK).

Full-color black

Black created by combining cyan, magenta, and yellow inks.

Halftone

A process used to reproduce an illustration, which involves breaking it up into small dots of different densities to simulate a full tonal range.

Holographic
Image made with a split laser beam that, when suitably illuminated, shows a three-dimensional image.

Metallix printing system
A printing system that does not require the use of metallized inks. Colors and metallic effects are built up using stochastic and halftone screening for different print elements, together with two registered varnishes, achieved inline.

Offset lithography
Method of printing using plates with image areas attracting ink and nonimage areas repelling ink. Nonimage areas may be coated with water to repel the oily ink or may have a surface, such as silicon, that repels ink.

Pantone
An international professional color-matching system, which includes colors created out of the four-color set, "special" individual colors, metallics, fluorescents, and pastels.

Pantone special
The term referring to a specific color recipe created by Pantone and described by a name or number.

Process colors
See Full color.

Screenprinting
A printing method that applies ink onto the surface of the material with a squeegee through a fine silk mesh. This achieves a much denser application of ink than lithography and may be used on an almost limitless variety of surfaces.

Spot color
A special color not generated by the four-color process method.

Tritone
Where three colors are printed together to make an image richer and denser in color.

Two passes of ink
Printing the same color twice, with the second pass of the press printing directly over the first to create a deeper, more intense, result.

Vegetable-based inks
Inks that are made with vegetable-based oils—as opposed to mineral-based, such as petroleum—and that are, as a result, more environmentally friendly.

Web-fed press
Printing press that prints onto a continuous roll of paper or plastic film. Printing is fast and can be applied to both sides of the material at once.

Finishing

Cut-and-stack labeling
Conventional method of labeling that delivers labels from a series of stacked flat sheets. Slower than the more modern and versatile reel-fed process.

Cutting form
See Die-cutting.

Debossing
Having a surface pattern pressed into the surface of the material. This process is also known as blind embossing.

Die-cutting
The method by which intricate shapes can be cut from cartonboard. This process requires a custom-made die, which has a sharp steel edge constructed to cut the required shape.

Embossing
Having a raised surface pattern. This is created by pressing the packaging material between a male and female form.

Etching
The process of marking a metal or glass surface by corrosion, usually acid.

Foil blocking
See Hot-foil stamping.

Hot-foil stamping
Application of heat and metallic film in
a specialty printing process that produces
a shiny design on paper, vinyl, textiles, wood,
hard plastic, leather, and other materials.
Foil stamping is also called hot stamping,
dry stamping, foil imprinting, or leaf stamping.

Lamination
The application of a clear matte or gloss
protective film over the printed surface of
a sheet of paper or card.

Laser cutting
A process that produces intricate cutting
through most materials using a laser beam.

Oxidative polymerization varnish
Varnish applied with an additional pass through
the press to provide barrier protection over
the printed surface. See also UV varnish.

Reel-fed labeling
Process of applying labels to containers from
a reel. Delivered at high speed, this process
allows a low-cost solution with superior
optical qualities.

"Soft-touch" varnish
A varnishing effect that has a light sponginess,
leaving a slight softness the surface to which
it is applied.

Spot varnish
See UV varnish.

UV varnish
A plastic-based varnish applied by screenprinting, available in matte, satin, and gloss
finishes. It can be applied over the entire
surface or treated as a spot varnish, enabling
the designer to print elements purely as
a varnish or to highlight selected elements
on the page.

FURTHER READING

Burgess, Paul, *Print and Production Finishes for CD + DVD Packaging*, RotoVision, 2006

Calver, Giles, *What is Packaging Design?*, RotoVision, 2007

Cliff, Stafford, *50 Trade Secrets of Great Design: Packaging*, Rockport, 2002

Fawcett-Tang, Roger and Mason, Daniel, *Experimental Formats and Packaging: Creative Solutions for Inspiring Graphic Design*, RotoVision, 2007

Fawcett-Tang, Roger, *Print and Production Finishes for Brochures and Catalogs*, RotoVision, 2008

Fishel, Catharine and King Gordon, Stacey, *Little Book of Big Packaging Ideas*, Rockport, 2007

Fishel, Catherine, *Mastering Materials, Bindings, and Finishes: The Art of Creative Production*, Rockport, 2007

Glaser, Jessica and Knight, Carolyn, *Print and Production Finishes for Bags, Labels and Point of Purchase*, RotoVision, 2008

Hampshire, Mark and Stephenson, Keith, *Packaging: Design Successful Packaging for Specific Customer Groups*, RotoVision, 2007

Herriott, Luke, *Designer's Packaging Bible: Creative Solutions for Outstanding Design*, RotoVision, 2007

Herriott, Luke, *The Packaging and Design Templates Sourcebook*, RotoVision, 2007

Hird, Kenneth, *Offset Lithographic Technology*, Goodheart-Wilcox, 2000

King Gordon, Stacey, *Packaging Makeover: Graphic Redesign for Market Change*, Rockport, 2007

Klimchuk, Marianne R. and Krasovec, Sandra A., *Packaging Design: Successful Product Branding from Concept to Shelf*, John Wiley & Sons, 2006

Kondo, Yoko, *Creative Gift Packaging*,
Japan Publications Trading, (2nd Edn) 2000

Michael Adams, J. and Dolin, Penny Ann,
Printing Technology, CENGAGE Delmar
Learning, 2007

Papanek, Victor, *The Green Imperative:
Ecology and Ethics in Design and Architecture*,
Thames and Hudson, 1995

Roth, László and Wybenga, George L.,
The Packaging Designer's Book of Patterns,
John Wiley & Sons, (3rd Edn) 2005

Victionary, *Printing Effects: An Exploration
of Printing Techniques*, Victionary, 2008

Witham, Scott, *Print and Production Finishes
for Promotional Items*, RotoVision, 2007

AGENCY INDEX

±
c/o Peter Crnokrak
116 Fulham Palace Road
Flat 423
London W6 9HH
UK
www.plusminus.ca

Boxal
www.boxal.com

Paul Cartwright Branding
53 Park Road
Ramsgate CT11 9TL
Kent
www.paulcartwrightbranding.co.uk

Chesapeake Corporation
Chesapeake Branded Packaging
Hollingwood Lane
Bradford BD7 2RQ
West Yorkshire
UK
www.chesapeakecorp.com

Chesapeake Packaging Systems
Chesapeake
Unit 14
Colthrop Business Park
Colthrop Lane
Thatcham RG19 4NB
Berkshire
UK
www.chesapeakecorp.com

Corigami Ltd.
Unit 1 Wharfedale Business Park
Shetcliffe Lane
Bradford BD4 9RS
West Yorkshire
UK
www.corigami.co.uk/6contact

Crown Food Europe
Perry Wood Walk
Worcester
Hereford and Worcester WR5 1EG
UK
www.crowncork.com

Crown Holdings, Inc.
One Crown Way
Philadelphia
PA 19154-4599
USA
www.crowncork.com

Davies Leslie-Smith
31 Hillfield Square
Chalfont St. Peter
Buckinghamshire SL9 0DY
UK
www.daviesleslie-smith.co.uk

Decanova
Toekomstlaan14
B-2200
Herentals
Belgium
www.deca.be
www.blikvangers.be

Design Bridge
18 Clerkenwell Close
London EC1R 0QN
UK
www.designbridge.com

Dragon Brands
1 Craven Hill
London W2 3EN
UK
www.dragonbrands.com

Dragon Rouge
32 Rue Pages
BP 83
92153 Suresnes Cedex
France
www.dragonrouge.com

Electric Design
Tong Hall
Tong Village
Bradford BD4 0RR
West Yorkshire
UK
www.electric-design.co.uk

Eurobox Envases Metálicos
Avenida Benidorm, 20
ES-03814 Benasau (Alicante)
Spain
www.euroboxenvases.com

CUC Nicolas Feuillatte
Chouilly BP210 F
51206 Epernay Cedex
France
www.feuillatte.com

Flipflop Design Ltd.
1st floor
No. 5 St. Catherines Terrace
Hove BN3 2RR
East Sussex
UK
www.flipflopdesign.co.uk

Geoplan Spatial Intelligence
Bilton Court
Wethorby Road
Harrogate HG3 1GP
UK
www.geoplan.com

Glud & Marstrand A/S
Hedenstedvej 14
DK-8723 Løsning
Denmark
www.glud-marstrand.com

Green House Design
Ginza East Altis 403
Tsukiji 1-12-5
Chuo-ku
Tokyo 104-0045
Japan
http://design-good.com

Gruppo ASA Metal Packagings
Strada dei Censiti 18/20
47891 Falciano E6
Republic of San Marino
www.gruppoasa.com

Helvetica
Minami-Aoyama 301
5-15-9
Minato-ku
Tokyo 107-0062
Japan
www.jkr.co.uk

Paul Hogarth
31 Warren Street
London W1T 5NG
UK
paul.hogarth@mac.com

Huhtamaki
Rowner Road
Gosport PO13 0PR
Hampshire
UK
www.huhtamaki.com

jkr Design Team/Jones Knowles Ritchie
128 Albert Street
London NW1 7NE
UK
www.jkr.co.uk

Jorge Jorge
Rua Fernál vas Dourado 62
4150-322 Porto
Portugal
www.jorgejorge.com

Andreas Kopp
Brühlmattweg 1
PO Box 207
CH-4107 Ettingen
Switzerland
www.andreaskopp.ch

**Mayr-Melnhof Packaging
International GmbH**
Brahmsplatz 6
A-1040 Vienna
Austria
www.mm-packaging.com

Parker Williams Design
1st Floor, Voysey House
Barley Mow Passage
London W4 4PT
UK
www.parkerwilliams.co.uk

pearlfisher
50 Brook Green
London W6 7BJ
UK
www.pearlfisher.com

27 West 24th Street
Suite 10e
New York
NY 10010
USA
www.pearlfisher.com

Pirlo GmbH & Co.
Hugo-Petters-Strasse 8–14
Kufstein 6330
Tirol
Austria
www.pirlo.com

Qualvis Print + Packaging
854 Melton Road
Thurmaston
Leicester LE4 8BT
UK
www.qualvis.co.uk

rlc | packaging group
Andertensche Wiese 18–25
30169 Hannover
Germany
www.rlc-packaging.com

Rexam
www.rexam.com

Rice Design
Greenhouse N204, 1-22-25
Soshigaya Setagaya-ku
Tokyo 157-0072
Japan
rice.d@w5.dion.ne.jp

Toyo Seikan
www.toyo-seikan.co.jp

Turnstyle
2219 NW Market Street
Seattle
WA 98107
USA
www.turnstylestudio.com

Vitro Packaging
5200 Tennyson Parkway
Suite 100 Plano
Texas 75024
USA
www.vitro.com

Waterform Design
30 Waterside Plaza 22c
New York
NY 10010
USA
www.masayonai.com

Webb Scarlett deVlam

12 Junction Mews
London W2 1PN
UK
www.wsdv.com

224 North Desplaines Suite 100S
Chicago
IL 60661
USA
www.wsdv.com

109/6 Cowper Wharf Road
Woolloomooloo
Sydney
NSW 2011
Australia
www.wsdv.com

Webtech

Killyhevlin Industrial Estate
Enniskillen
Co. Fermanagh BT74 4EJ
Northern Ireland
www.webtechni.com

West Island Group

Afton Road
Freshwater PO37 7A11
Isle of Wight
UK
www.westisland.co.uk

Whitespace

7/8 Randolph Place
Edinburgh EH3 7TE
UK
www.whitespacers.com

INDEX

ABOUT THE AUTHOR

Edward Denison writes regularly about subjects across a wide range of design disciplines and has received critical acclaim for his written and photographic work through numerous printed and broadcast media internationally. His published works for RotoVision include *Packaging Prototypes: Design Fundamentals*, *Packaging Prototypes: Thinking Green*, and *More Packaging Prototypes*.